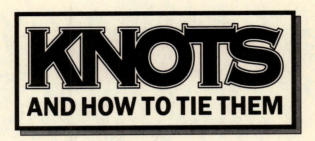

KNOTS
AND HOW TO TIE THEM

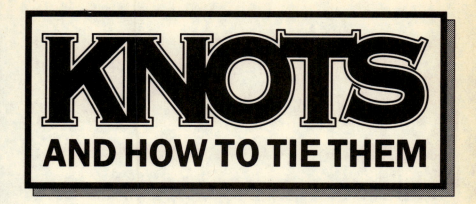

KNOTS
AND HOW TO TIE THEM

Revised
by
Walter B. Gibson

WINGS BOOKS
New York • Avenel, New Jersey

Copyright © 1989, 1984, 1978, 1961 by Walter Brown Gibson

This edition is published by Wings Books,
distributed by Random House Value Publishing, Inc.,
40 Engelhard Avenue, Avenel, New Jersey 07001,
by arrangement with Lifetime Books, Inc.

Random House
New York • Toronto • London • Sydney • Auckland

Manufactured in the United States of America

Library of Congress Cataloging-in-Publication Data
Gibson, Walter Brown, 1897-
        [Fell's official guide to knots and how to tie them]
        Knots and how to tie them / by Walter B. Gibson.
            p.   cm.
        Originally published : Fell's official guide to knots and how to
    tie them.   1961.
        Includes index.
        ISBN 0-517-09369-3
        1. Knots and Splices.   I. Title.
    VM533.G5   1993
    623.88'82—DC20   93-8134
                                                              CIP

8 7 6 5 4 3 2

CONTENTS

I
KNOTS ARE KNOTS

Knots are Knots

Few things are easier than making a knot in a piece of string or rope. Although, how good or efficient that knot may be is another story. Some people just can't seem to tie knots that will stay, while others have an aptitude for tying knots that just won't come untied, no matter how hard they work at it.

Someone once quipped, "Almost everybody knows how to tie a knot, but practically nobody knows how to tie one right." That is very nearly true. At least 99 percent of the population knows how to tie a knot of some sort; and of those, at least 99 percent do it blindly or by rote, unless they have had some instruction or have made a study of rope work.

"Of course I know how to tie knots!" a person might insist. "It's one of the first things I was taught." And probably, that lesson was the last, given by an instructor who had been similarly taught — the wrong way. If a survey were taken, it would probably prove that the greatest hazard to human safety, aside from driving in holiday traffic or rocking a boat filled with people who cannot swim, is not knowing how to tie a knot properly.

Consider the thousands of instances where people have tripped over trailing shoelaces, where scaffoldings or other weights have slipped from insecure fastenings, or when anything from a mad dog to a cabin cruiser has broken loose from its moorings, and you get the general idea. On the other side are the rare instances where a life has been spared because somebody bungled the tying of a hangman's noose.

This suggests another important factor in rope work — it is possible to tie a knot properly only to find that it is the wrong knot for the purpose. Actually, this may be worse than tying the right knot the wrong way, because the mistake is seldom recognized until it is too late. Knots that hold under some conditions will slip under others. This is a basic principle of rope work, and also one of the most intriguing things about the art.

All ties or fastenings that use rope or cordage fall into three general classifications: knots, hitches, and bends. All are "knots" in the full sense of the term, and there are some ties which have more than one classification, their purposes being interchangeable.

A *knot*, in the restricted sense, is a tie made in a rope and usually requires the manipulation of only one end. Both ends may be used when the rope is short enough.   A *hitch* is used primarily for attaching a rope to another object — a post, ring, or what have you. This may automatically result in the formation of a knot. Conversely, a knot may be converted to a hitch.

A *bend* involves joining of two ropes so they will stand the strain of being used as one long rope. Obviously, this can be done by merely knotting the ends together. But a bend, in its fullest meaning, signifies a "bending" or "binding" of ropes to eliminate their slipping, particularly when they are of different size or make-up.

The classification of the tie is less important than the purpose it serves, or its correct formation. Loosely speaking, you begin your "knotting" with a single rope end, throw a "hitch" when you attach it to an object, and "bend" two ropes together. But, the practical way is to begin at the beginning, namely with the loose end of the rope and the simpler ways of knotting it.

II
SIMPLE KNOTS

Basic Knot Formations

In basic knot work, three terms are used to indicate different portions of the rope.

First, there is the loose or working end of the rope, which is used in forming simple knots and is referred to as the *End*.

Next is the slack portion of the rope which can be bent until it practically doubles back on itself, and is known as the *Bight*.

Finally, there is the leftover or unused section of the rope which includes the longer end. This is commonly called the *Standing Part*.

At the outset, you actually only have the working end and the standing part. If the rope is drawn taut between the hands, you have two ends ("A" and "B") with a length of rope between, "A" being the working end and "B" the standing part.

The moment you allow any slack, a bight begins to form between the end and the standing part (fig. 1), but it is not truly a bight unless retained in the doubled form.

However, if the sides are crossed, it becomes a Loop (fig. 2). There are two types: the Overhand Loop, where the end is carried over or above the standing part of the rope; or the Underhand Loop, where the end goes under or beneath the standing part. (fig. 3)

When a loop is carried around the standing part, it is called a Turn, or Round Turn. Thus, to "take a turn" around the standing part is almost the same as forming an "overhand" loop followed by an "underhand" loop.

These various formations are combined in one way or another to produce a knot, which results when the end of the rope is properly interwoven or inserted through a waiting loop.

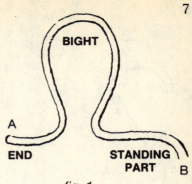

BIGHT

A

END

STANDING PART

B

fig. 1

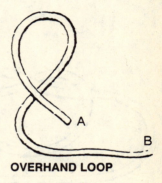

A

B

OVERHAND LOOP

fig. 2

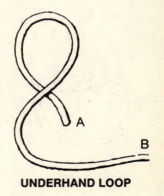

A

B

UNDERHAND LOOP

Overhand Knot

Form a loop by crossing the end over the standing part of the rope. Draw the end upward through the loop thus formed. This makes a solid knot when drawn tight, the sort that may be used to prevent the end of a rope from unraveling.

Note that if you start with an overhand loop, you bring the end up through to complete the knot; with an underhand loop you push the end down through the loop to form the knot.

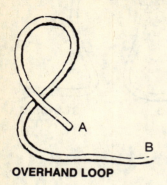

OVERHAND LOOP

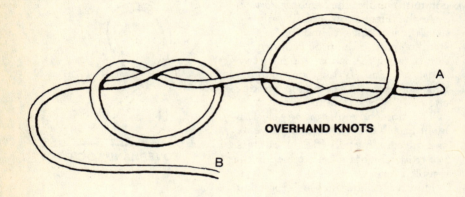

OVERHAND KNOTS

Double or Triple Overhand

Simply continue the ordinary Overhand Knot by bringing the end over the loop, then push it through, as many times as desired. Done twice, it gives you a double knot; three times, a triple; four times, a quadruple; and so on, however far you want to go. Tightened, this becomes a very solid knot.

Figure Eight

Bend the bight of the rope until it crosses the standing part, forming an overhand loop (fig. 1). Then bend the end of the rope in the opposite direction to form an underhand loop below the first, giving the appearance of a figure "8" or the character "&" when the free end is considered (fig. 2).

Push the end down through the overhand loop and the knot will be complete (fig. 3).

Drawn tight, the Figure Eight is a larger and better "stopper" than the simple Overhand Knot. This is also called a "Flemish Knot."

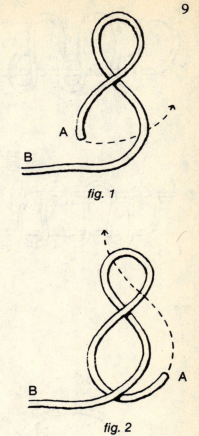

fig. 1

fig. 2

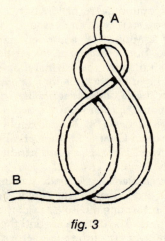

fig. 3

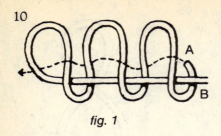

fig. 1

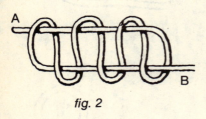

fig. 2

Multiple Figure Eight

This is a fancier bit of rope work. As the name implies, it is a series of Figure Eights that can be "set up" by forming the first loop, then alternating underhand and overhand loops in left-right, left-right fashion (fig. 1).

Then thread the end up through the loop on the right. Weave it over the bottom portion and under the top portion of each loop, continuing until you push it down through the top or original loop, exactly as in the simple Figure Eight (fig. 2).

Draw on the end and the standing part, and you will form overlapping eights.

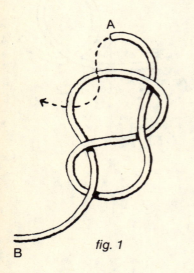

fig. 1

Stevedore's Knot

There are several variations of this knot, but one of the simplest is a combination of the Figure Eight with the common Overhand Knot.

You start with an overhand loop and continue with an underhand loop. But, when the end is pushed down through the original loop (as in the Figure Eight) it is then brought over it and under it again (fig. 1), so that an Overhand Knot is tied to the original loop (fig. 2). It is double the size of an Overhand Knot or a Figure Eight, so it makes a good handle on a heavy rope.

A similar knot is made starting with an ordinary Figure Eight, but when forming the lower underhand loop, take a full turn around the standing part of the rope before pushing the end down through the first loop. This will tighten in the same fashion. With either version, added turns may be used.

Stevedore's Knot (continued)

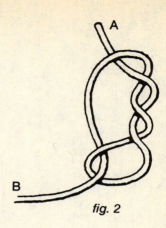

fig. 2

Eye Knot

This is an effective way of forming a strong loop. Take a bight in a rope, hold the two strands together and tie them in a simple Overhand Knot, allowing a portion of the bight to extend like a loop.

Pull the knot tight, making the loop whatever size you require. The loop can be put over a post and any pull on the doubled rope will tighten the knot still more.

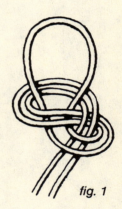

fig. 1

Figure Eight Eye Knot

In this case, the bight is tied in a Figure Eight knot, a portion being left extended as a loop. Though bulkier and more cumbersome than the simpler Overhand type of Eye Knot, this one is designed to stand more strain on the knotted portion of the rope.

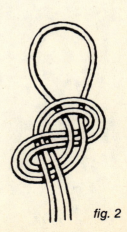

fig. 2

III
DOUBLE KNOTS

"Two Rope" Square Knot

Seldom, if ever, has the peculiar
construction of the Square Knot (or
Reef Knot) been properly analyzed.
This knot can be formed solely by the
union of two bights, nothing more.
That's right — you use a bight.

Take the exact center of the long
rope, and form the center into a
downward bight (fig. 1.)

fig. 1

Take one end of the short (ten
inch) rope and insert it through the
bight from front to back, and right to
left. Then, carry it across in front of
the neck and narrow portion of the
bight (fig. 2.)

Thrust that same end through the
bight, this time from front to back,
bringing it out the left side of the
bight, as you view it (fig. 3.)

fig. 2

Get the short rope "middled" and
pull the ends of both ropes. The
result is instantaneous and obvious
(fig. 4). You have a Square Knot
formed by two bights.

Note that the ropes hold strongly
in that position. Nothing could be
stronger at the middle of a rope. If
they cause trouble, it's always when
an end is too close.

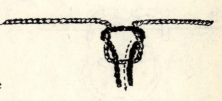

fig. 3

You will observe, too, that the
bights can be loosened by simply
pushing them toward each other. The
operation of this knot, so simplified,
is of value in the study of the more
complicated knots that will now be
discussed.

fig. 4

Square Knot or Sailor's Knot

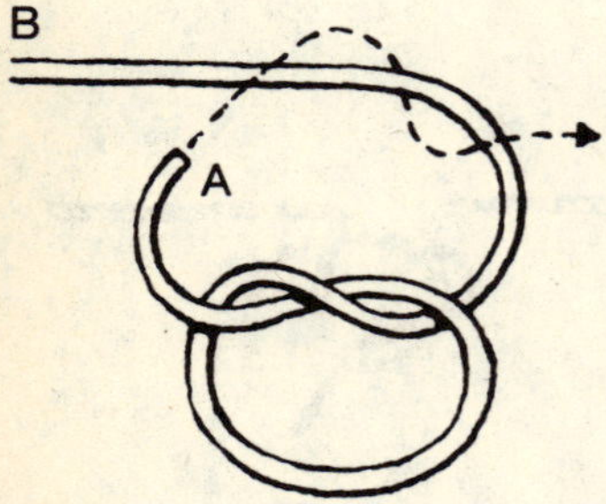

One of the easiest knots to tie and the best knot for certain purposes, the Square Knot is simply two Overhand Knots. But, be careful when tying, otherwise, the knot will go wrong.

The rule is this: If you begin the first knot by forming an overhand loop, do the same with the second knot (fig. 1). Or, in other words, if you cross the end in front of the standing part to tie the first knot, do it the same way for the second (fig. 2).

This applies when using a single end to form the Square Knot. When tying two ends of a short rope, it is just as well to work with one end, so as to keep the rule in mind.

The Square Knot is sometimes appropriately called the "Flat Knot" because it actually flattens when pulled tight (fig. 3).

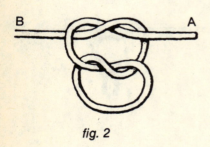

fig. 1

fig. 2

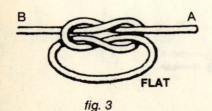

FLAT

fig. 3

The Granny Knot

This is simply a mistaken form of the Square Knot; the rule of keeping the same end front is not applied.

When you tighten a Granny, its make-up is easily noted in a rope, because it fails to pull flat, one half being tied forward, the other half backwards, so to speak (fig. 3).

Often, a Granny Knot will jam, making it difficult to untie. Or, in perverse fashion, it may slip instead of remaining tied. For this reason, the Granny has been branded "the most dangerous of knots," though it does not quite deserve that stigma.

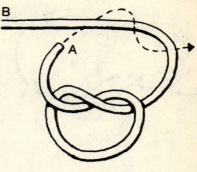

fig. 1

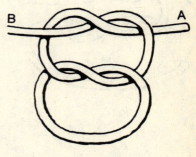

fig. 2

fig. 3

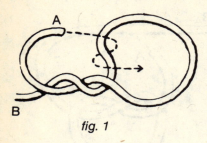

fig. 1

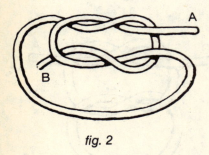

fig. 2

Rogue's Knot

Due to its odd formation, this knot is rarely tied by accident. It lives up to its name as a knot that may be purposely used to make the ends of a rope pull apart. This gives it value as a "trick" knot; otherwise, it is useless as well as dangerous.

The Rogue's Knot looks like a Square Knot and is tied in a similar way, but with this difference. The long end ("B") is bent back on itself before the working end ("A") is tied on to it (fig. 1). Thus, with the first Overhand Knot, the ends point in the same direction. When the second Overhand is tied on top, they point opposite each other, as they should (fig. 2).

As a result, one end is below the other, so when strain is put on the standing part, by drawing it two ways, the knot yields and pulls apart. So, to make sure that a Square Knot is safe, it is wise to study the ends and note their position.

Surgeon's Knot

This is simply an elaboration of the Square Knot. You begin with a Double Overhand; then, reverse the ends and tie a single Overhand on top. By giving the first knot the extra turn, it tends to hold while the second is being added. The single Overhand is sufficient on top, but the knot can be "evened" by adding a "double" if desired.

Such a knot is useful in tying packages as well as in surgery, from which it gets its name.

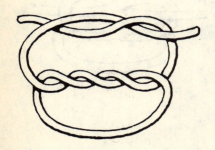

Bow Knot

One of the simplest and most useful knots, this is handy when it is necessary to undo the knot quickly.

The Single Bow is a variation of the Square Knot, in which the working end ("A") is tied about the standing part ("B") or another rope end. Begin with a simple Overhand Knot, then take a bight in the standing part and tie the working end around it, forming the second knot (fig. 1).

You then have the equivalent of a Square Knot except that one end ("B") is doubled back through the upper half of the knot. This can be tightened like a Square Knot. To undo it, simply pull on end "B," reducing the formation to a single Overhand Knot (fig. 2).

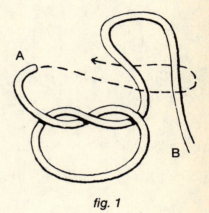

fig. 1

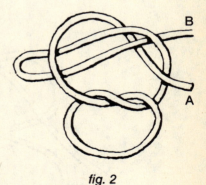

fig. 2

Double Bow

This may be tied in either of two ways. The first and preferable method is to start exactly as with the Single Bow Knot, allowing a fair amount of length to the working end. Tie the first Overhand Knot.

In tying the second Overhand, form a bight in "B," but instead of pushing end "A" through the new loop, draw a bight through, so that "A" becomes identical with "B" in formation. When it is drawn tight, you have two loops instead of one. A pull on either end ("A" or "B") will undo the knot.

The alternate method is tie a Single Overhand, then form identical bights in "A" and "B." The bights themselves are then tied in an Overhand Knot on top of the first one. It results in the same formation, but is a little slower.

The Double Bow is the familiar Shoestring or Shoelace Knot. Everyone is familiar with it, but it can be tied in either the "right" way or the "wrong" way. The right way is to follow the pattern of the Square Knot. It will go wrong if the ends are reversed in tying, as with the Granny Knot.

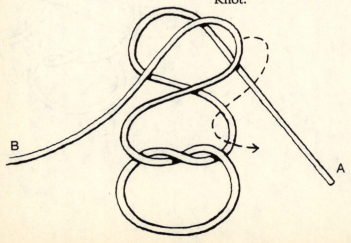

Shoestring Specials

There are two effective ways for keeping shoestrings tight. One is to use the two ends to tie an added Overhand Knot on top of the bow (fig. 1). The other is to form another pair of bights in "A" and "B," tying them as a second bow on top of the first (fig's 2 & 3).

In each case, make sure the added knot follows the proper direction. It takes longer to undo these knots, as the upper one must be untied in order to get at the bow, but they stay tight while in use.

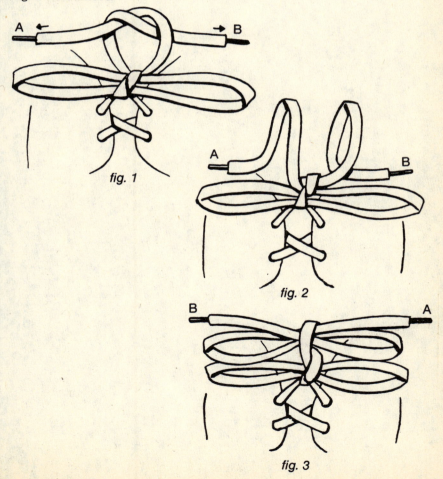

fig. 1

fig. 2

fig. 3

IV
HITCHES

About Hitches

A hitch, as its name implies, is a means of hitching a rope to an object, often in a temporary way, so that it can be undone or removed quite readily.

Some knots can be used as hitches, as can some bends. But sailors think of "bending" a rope rather than "hitching" it, when making a rope fast to an object.

One advantage of a hitch is that it can be made directly about an object — such as a post, pole or spar -- instead of having to be formed first, like a knot, and then placed over the object. Most hitches are specially designed to "fall apart" when the object is removed. In short, they are not knots, because they have to be made fast to an object in order to exist.

Crossing Hitch

This simple formation might well be called the "Loop Hitch," for that is exactly what it is, a loop that is held together as a hitch.

If you carry the end of a rope around an object and across the standing part, then exert opposite pressure so that one portion of the rope draws upon the other, you will have the simple Crossing Hitch.

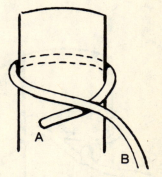

This is useful in tying packages along with other things, and it answers the purpose of a knot, provided the ends of the rope are otherwise secured.

This "loop hitch" can be used as a "one end" fastening by forming a loop around an object so that the loose end is jammed between the standing part and the object. A pull in one direction will tighten the loop and hold it in place.

Half Hitch

In its simplest form, the Half Hitch is made by looping a rope around a post or other upright object, bringing the end around the standing part to take a partial turn, and pulling them in opposite directions, so that the rope tightens there (fig. 1).

However, to make the Half Hitch hold on its own, you must bring the end up and around the standing part, then tuck it down between the rope and the post, so that it will jam there when the loop is tightened (fig. 2).

Actually, this is the same as a simple Overhand Knot dropped over the post, because your "hitch" now has become a "knot." The chief difference is that you can hitch the rope to a tree, fence, metal ring, or any object where the knot cannot be dropped on from the top.

The Half Hitch is a basic rope formation important to others that follow.

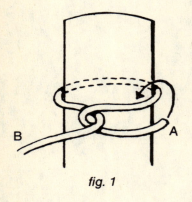

B   A

fig. 1

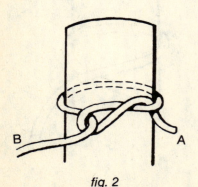

B   A

fig. 2

Timber Hitch

So called because it can be used for
rolling logs or hoisting lumber, the
Timber Hitch is useful as a temporary
hitch that will hold while needed and
loosen easily.

It is simply a Half Hitch with this
added twist: After drawing the end
down through the loop, bring it over
and under the side of the loop again,
so that it jams more firmly. It thus
becomes a double Overhand Knot,
and further turns can be taken to
triple or quadruple it, if so desired.

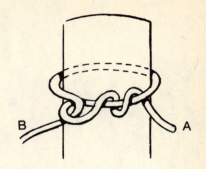

Timber Hitch with Half Hitch

This is used for hauling long
objects, such as beams, in an upright
fashion. First, form a simple Half
Hitch above the center of the object,
by making an overhand loop and
drawing the end well down, while the
standing part goes straight up.

Allow enough bight below the Half
Hitch to form a Timber Hitch around
the lower portion of the object,
tightening the free end with the
customary double twist. Hoist the
object with the standing part of the
rope.

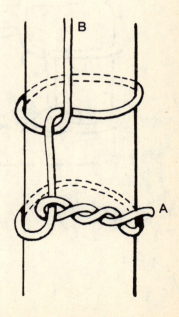

Killick Hitch

This gets its name from a "killick," a block of stone used as an anchor for a small boat. Sometimes the stone is encased in a loose "crate," but the hitch is the same in either case.

The Killick Hitch is practically the same as the Half Hitch and the Timber Hitch combined, but usually a few more turns are taken with the rope end, some extra length being allowed for this.

Since it is used in water, the rope tends to swell, making this a permanent fastening rather than a temporary job.

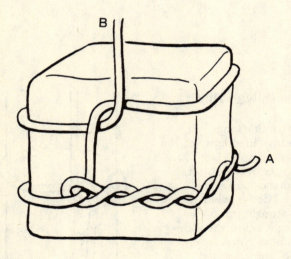

Fisherman's Bend

Although called a bend, this would more correctly be called a hitch. It is one of the strongest fastenings in that category.

You begin by taking two round turns about the post or other object to which you are affixing the rope. Using the rope end, take a Half Hitch about the standing part, then draw the end beneath the two round turns and tighten it. Then, take another Half Hitch around the standing part and draw the end tight in the usual fashion.

Experiments with this hitch will demonstrate its ability to stand strain. This bend is also known as the "Anchor Bend."

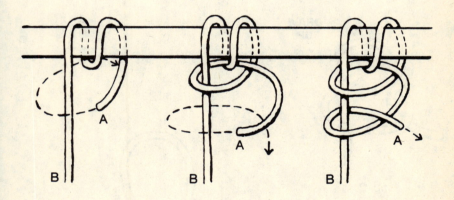

Simple Slip Knot

Also known as the Running Knot or Running Overhand, this is tied much like the single Overhand Knot.

The end is held stationary in the left hand while the right hand uses the standing part to form an overhand loop and draw the rope up through (fig. 1). But, having no end to draw, the right hand must use a bight instead (fig. 2).

The left hand tightens the knot by pulling on the end (fig. 3), and the bight then forms a noose or loop that can be drawn to any size by slipping it through the knot. When desired, the knot can instantly be untied by pulling the standing part down through, knot and all.

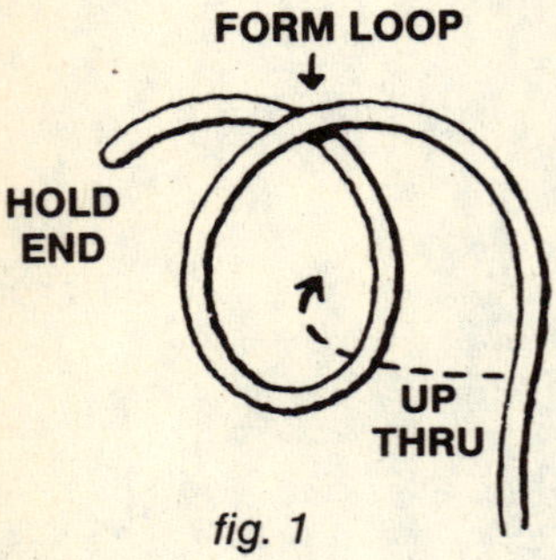

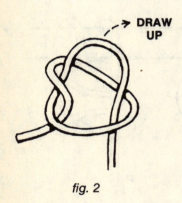

FORM LOOP

HOLD END

UP THRU

fig. 1

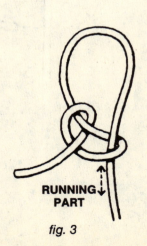

DRAW UP

fig. 2

RUNNING PART

fig. 3

Double Slip Knot

The Simple Slip Knot is, in effect, a Single Bow Knot; the "bow" being the loop or bight. You can tie a Double Slip Knot or Double Bow in the center of a long rope by forming an overhand loop (as shown in fig. 1) and drawing a bight up through it with the right hand, while the left presses a bight down through it (fig. 2). Pull both loops through, thus tightening the knot between them and the Double Bow results (fig. 3). By drawing on the single portions of the rope, the knot is quickly undone.

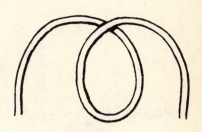

fig. 1

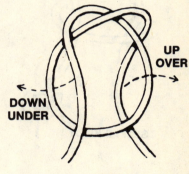

UP OVER

DOWN UNDER

fig. 2

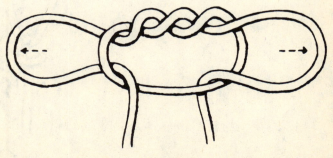

fig. 3

Slippery Hitch

Start by tying a Running Knot in the loose end of the rope (instead of the standing part), near the end (fig. 1). The knot is formed around the end portion of the rope.

If the loop is drawn up, the end will come out through. To prevent that, tie an ordinary Overhand Knot — or two or three —near the end of the rope (fig. 1). This serves as a "stopper" when it is drawn up to the Slip Knot (fig. 2). The result is the true Slippery Hitch. The loop can be "hitched" over a post and will not pull out, thanks to the combination.

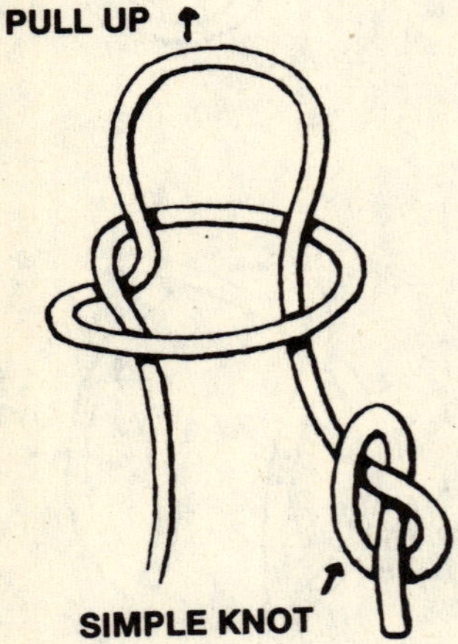

PULL UP ↑

SIMPLE KNOT

fig. 1

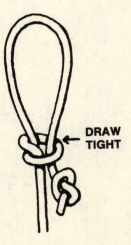

DRAW TIGHT ←

fig. 2

Running Knot and Half Hitch

With this combination, you again tie the knot around the standing part, so that the short end slips through freely. Then take the end below the knot and carry it around behind the standing part to the front, where it is tucked down through the loop, producing a Half Hitch (fig. 2). Drawing the loop up pulls the Half Hitch into the Running Knot. The loop can be adjusted to almost any size and used as a "hitch" over a post or similar object.

This is comparable to the Slippery Hitch.

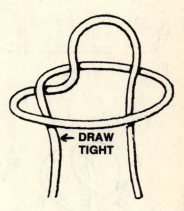

← DRAW TIGHT

fig. 1

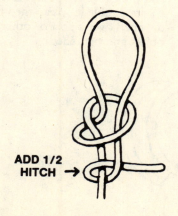

ADD 1/2 HITCH →

fig. 2

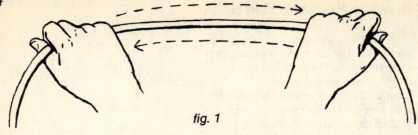

fig. 1

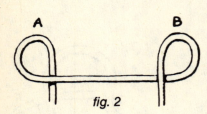

A   B

fig. 2

Clove Hitch

Once you acquire the knack, you can make this hitch in what amounts to a single, automatic operation.

Hold the rope in the left hand, slightly to the right of the center. The left hand is tilted downward, its back turned outward. Now, bring the right hand across in back of the left and grip the rope in the same fashion but to the left of the center (fig. 1).

Sweep the right hand to the right and the left hand to the left, so they assume their natural positions (fig. 2). At the same time turn the right hand palm upward. Twist the loose left fist rightward and downward, planting its knuckles squarely in the half-opened right palm (fig. 3).

Grip both coils with the right hand and the Clove Hitch is formed (fig. 4). Its double loop can then be dropped over a post or other upright object and tightened.

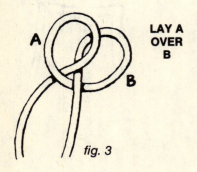

A   LAY A
           OVER
           B
        B

fig. 3

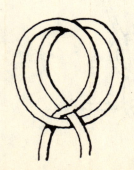

fig. 4

Midshipman's Hitch

This is simply two Half Hitches, but with an added twist to one. The easiest procedure is as follows: Use the end of the rope to take a Half Hitch around the standing part; then follow with the second Half Hitch, but in completing it, make a round turn about the standing part (fig. 1), before drawing the end through the loop (fig 2).

An alternate method is to make the round turn in completing the first Half Hitch; then simply add the second Half Hitch in the accepted fashion.

In either case, the Midshipman's Hitch does not have to be looped about an object to use it; it can be made and adjusted like a noose and will "stay put" when drawn tight.

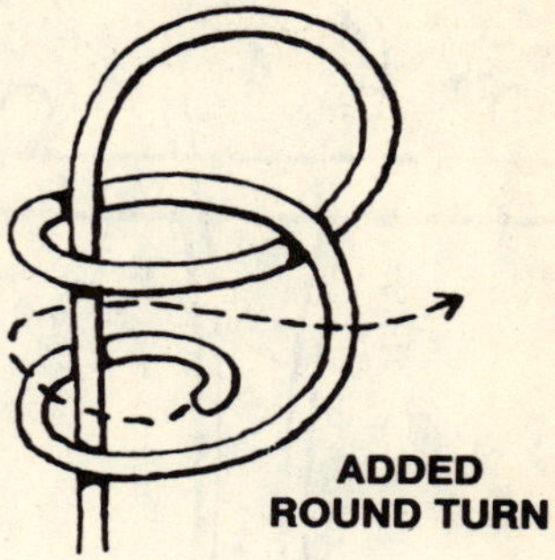

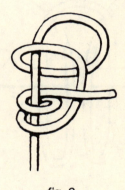

ADDED ROUND TURN

fig. 1

fig. 2

ALTERNATE METHOD

ROUND TURN ↓

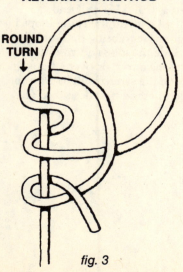

fig. 3

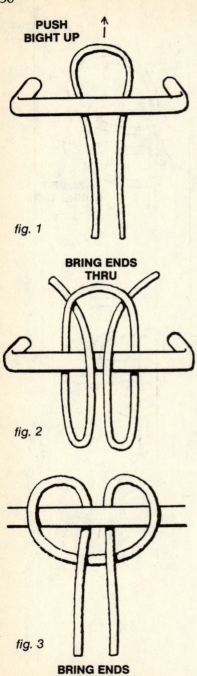

PUSH BIGHT UP

fig. 1

BRING ENDS THRU

fig. 2

fig. 3

BRING ENDS DOWN THRU

Lark's Head

Also known as the "Baggage Tag Loop" and the "Cow Hitch," because of its varied uses, this is very easy to make.

With a short rope, take a bight in the center and push the doubled rope up through a ring, trunk handle or some similar object (fig. 1). Bring the ends of the rope around the attachment and thrust them through the bight or center loop (fig. 2). Pull the ends taut and the job is done (fig. 3).

For hitching a rope to a post or a rod, you have a slight problem, which is easily solved if one end of the post is "open" or free. Here we assume that one end of the rope is already attached, say to an animal that is tethered, or that the rope is a very long one and that you want to hitch it at the center. In this case, place the rope across the open hands, which are held palms upward (fig. 1). Turn the hands inward, toward each other, gripping the rope loosely, to form two loops with a bight between (fig. 2). At this stage, you have what is termed a "False Lark's Head."

To make it real, twist the loops just enough more to bring them side by side. Slide the loops down over a post, along a rod, or over a hook and you have the same result as with the simpler method first described (fig. 3).

FALSE LARK'S HEAD

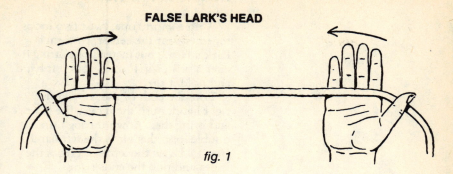

fig. 1

TWIST

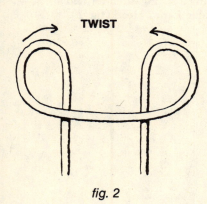

fig. 2

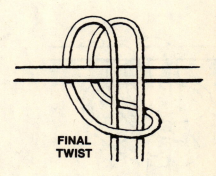

FINAL TWIST

fig. 3

Double Lark's Head

With a short rope, twist two loops together near the center, to form a Lark's Head, but instead of putting it over a post, slip it onto your left hand and hold it there.

Take the ends of the rope in the right hand, push them over the bar and bring them down through the double loop that girds the left hand (fig. 1). Draw the left hand from the ropes and pull the ends tight.

The result is one Lark's Head passing through another at right angles, forming a strong hitch termed a "Double Lark's Head (fig. 2).

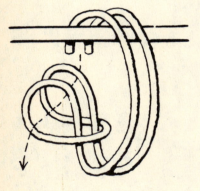

fig. 1

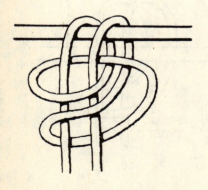

fig. 2

Triple or Interlocking Lark's Head

This is often called the "Triple Lark's Head" because it consists of adding two loops to the simple Lark's Head, one on each side, to make three in all. Actually, the term "interlocking" is more appropriate because the result is a chain that can be extended as long as the rope holds out.

Start with a simple Lark's Head, using a short rope, so the ends can be drawn through a bight that has been looped over a ring, or preferably a chair rung or short bar. The two ends are brought through the loop from the back so that they emerge below the bar.

Now, carry the right end up in front of the bar, toward the right; bring it over the bar, down in back and out to the front (fig. 1), drawing it through the loop thus formed and pulling it tight from in front (fig. 2). Do the same with the left end of the rope, but in the opposite direction, working toward the left.

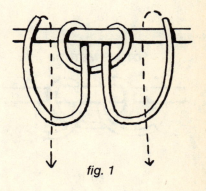

fig. 1

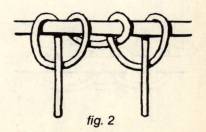

fig. 2

That's one way of doing it, particularly if you want to add more loops in the same fashion. But if you want to wind up with a Triple Lark's Head and no more, you can vary it thus: Take each end of the rope up in back of the bar, over the top, down in front and through the loop toward the back (fig. 1). This brings two strands side by side and forms two conventional hitches, which are "squared off" so to speak, with the third or original hitch between them (fig. 2).

In making a multiple hitch, of five, seven, nine or more interlocking loops, you can use the first process (up in front, down in back) until you come to the final pair. Then square them off by the reverse procedure.

To form an Interlocking Lark's Head in the center of the rope: Hold the rope across the hands, palms up, and twist them together to form the False Lark's Head. Retain this with the left hand while the right gathers additional coils, twisting each one inward. Grip this with the right hand while the left gathers its extra coils, also working inward. Slide the loops onto the end of the bar and that's it.

To "square off" the final loops, simply twist them outward instead of inward. The same can be done with the final loops of a longer chain.

OTHER METHOD

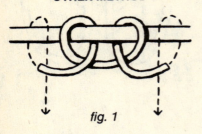

fig. 1

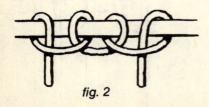

fig. 2

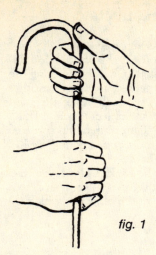

fig. 1

Crossed Lark's Head

In forming this variation, place the rope across the palm of the right hand, with the fingers pointing toward the left, so that the right hand can grip the rope in a loose fist.

A little below that, the left hand grips the rope in similar fashion, but palm downward, with its fingers pointing toward the right (fig. 1).

Now, twist the hands in the same direction, in this case toward the left, so that each hand forms a loop in its portion of the rope. These loops will be "opposites" — one an overhand, the other an underhand (fig. 2).

Bring the loops side by side (fig. 3); slide them together over a post or a hook. The Crossed Lark's Head is the result (fig. 4).

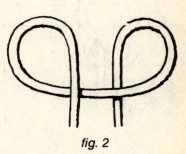

fig. 2

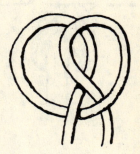

fig. 3

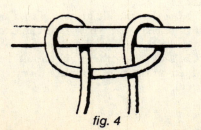

fig. 4

(ONE INWARD TWIST)

fig. 1

(TWO INWARD TWISTS)

fig. 2

(3 INWARD TWISTS)

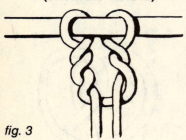

fig. 3

Racking Hitch

This is an extension of the Lark's Head as formed from the double loops (fig. 1). Before bringing the loops together, give them another twist toward each other; then slide them on the object (fig. 2). This forms a tighter hitch and spreads the strain on the rope making the hitch more reliable.

Like the Larks's Head, the Racking Hitch falls apart as soon as drawn clear from the object to which it is attached.

Cat's-paw

More twists are added, loop to loop —three, four, five or whatever number you wish — to form the Cat's-paw, which this hitch somewhat resembles in appearance. With a twisted rope, this should be done against the "lay" or "twist," adding more strength proportionately (fig.3).

Ordinarily, both loops of the Cat's-paw are slipped over the same object, but they can be attached separately, say to two hooks that are set a short distance apart. The double-twist portion of the rope then serves as a sort of hanger, running between the hooks.

Note that the illustration shows an unbalanced "Cat's-paw" with an extra twist on the left. In the standard "Cat's-paw" another twist should be added on the right, to make them equal.

V

BENDS AND KNOTS FOR JOINING ROPE ENDS

Knotty Alternatives

The familiar Square Knot or Reef Knot, though often used for tying the ends of two ropes together, is actually a poor knot for that purpose. Aside from the risk of mistakenly tying a Granny, or worse, a Rogue's Knot, the Square Knot can be converted into a Slip Knot if one rope is drawn straight by pulling on both the end and standing part.

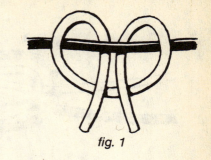

fig. 1

The "knot" then becomes a simple Lark's Head in one rope, hitched over another rope, as shown in figure 1. As such, it can be slid off the end of the other rope, if the end happens to be loose.

This can be used, however, as a method for affixing the center of a short rope to that of a longer one, by simply working in reverse, as follows: Take a bight in the center of a short rope. Bring it up in back of the long rope and down over the front. Bring the ends of the short rope up through the loop thus formed and draw them taut (fig. 2). To convert this into a Square Knot, press the bight upward and draw the two strands of the longer rope in that same direction, keeping them together (fig. 3).

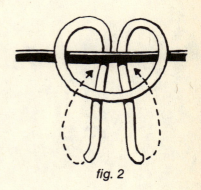

fig. 2

In joining two rope ends, the Square Knot becomes still more risky if the ropes are of different size, material or finish. Here, a Square Knot is less likely to hold than other knots commonly used as joins. Even with all things being equal — ropes included — the very formation of the Square Knot, or its halfsized edition the Overhand Knot, reduces the strength of the rope to 50 percent or less.

Other types of knots, bends and hitches show a much higher efficiency, holding ability and adaptability toward meeting strain, that gives them special merit as rope joiners. These form the subject of this chapter.

fig. 3

fig. 1

Double Overhand

A quick, sure way of tying the ends of two ropes together is to lay the ends side by side and tie them as one (fig. 1), by means of an ordinary Overhand Knot. When this is tightened and the standing parts of the two ropes are pulled in opposite directions, the knot becomes very firm (fig. 2).

This knot, though it will never slip, is cumbersome and bulky in appearance.

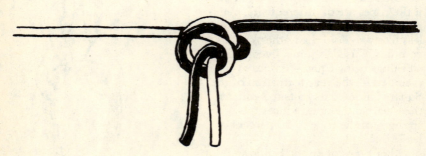

fig. 2

Ordinary Knot

Though formed by two simple knots, this is not as "ordinary" as its name would imply. However, its formation is an easy one to follow.

Take one rope and tie a loose Overhand Knot near one end. Take the other rope and bring it end to end with the first (fig. 1).

Pushing it backward through the knot, follow the direction of the first rope (fig. 2).

Thus the second rope end is tied in an identical knot, headed the other way (fig. 3).

When the end of the second rope emerges, pull the two knots tight and they become the Ordinary Knot.

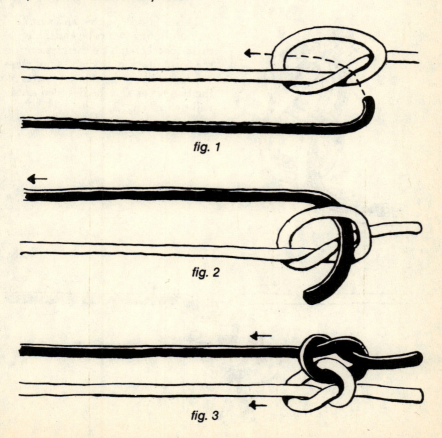

fig. 1

fig. 2

fig. 3

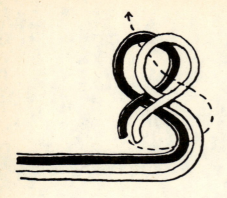

fig. 1

Flemish Knot

This is another quick and simple way of joining two rope ends. Lay them together and tie them as one in the form of a Figure Eight Knot (fig's 1 & 2). Pull on the standing parts of the two ropes and the doubled knot will tighten (fig. 3).

fig. 2

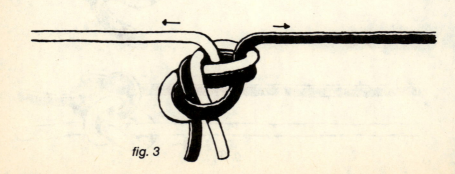

fig. 3

fig. 1

Figure Eight Hand Knot

A neater knot can be formed by first tying a Figure Eight in one rope end, then "following back" through the loose knot with the end of the second rope (fig's 1 & 2). This is also called a Flemish Knot but it is better termed the Figure Eight Hand Knot.

fig. 2

Sheet Bend

This method of joining two ropes of different sizes is stronger than the commonly used Square Knot. It also can be used for tying ropes of the same size or two ends of a single rope.

The tie is simplicity itself. Take a bight near the end of one rope and hold it in position with the left thumb and fingers (fig. 1). The right hand grips the other rope end and throws a Half Hitch around the bight (fig. 2).

Then, instead of tucking the loose end under the standing part of the rope, the right hand pushes it through the bight held by the left (fig. 3). Pull the ropes tight and the Sheet Bend is completed.

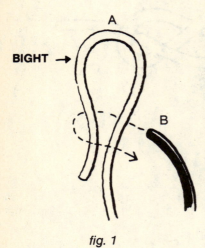

BIGHT →

A

B

fig. 1

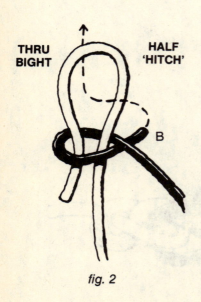

THRU BIGHT

HALF 'HITCH'

B

fig. 2

fig. 3

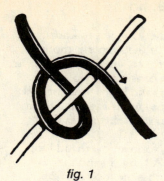

fig. 1

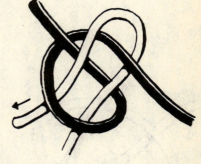

fig. 2

Weaver's Knot

The Weaver's Knot is practically identical with the Sheet Bend, the difference being the manner in which the knot is tied, weavers using a process suited to the joining of two threads.

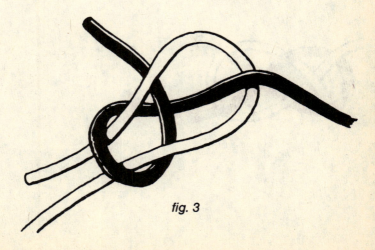

fig. 3

Carrick Bend

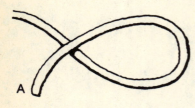

fig. 1

One of the strongest of knots, this is also one of the simplest, though it may not seem so when you first try it. Actually, it consists of two interwoven overhand loops, one formed by each rope end. It is getting them into that position that poses the problem.

To start, form an overhand loop with end "A" (fig. 1) and then lay end "B" across the loop (fig. 2). From then on, end "B" is worked under and over each successive rope strand, to form the linking loop, as indicated by the arrow in figure 2.

Where you may go wrong with the Carrick Bend is at the very start. The end of the second rope, "B", must go over both portions of the loop formed by the first rope, "A". (It would seem that it should alternate in "over-under" fashion, which it does, but not until end "B" is brought into position.) (fig. 3)

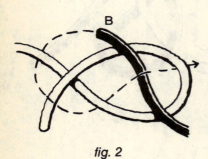

fig. 2

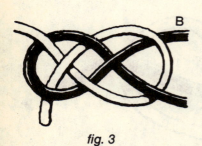

fig. 3

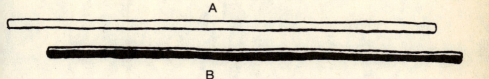

A

B

fig. 1

The English Knot

Though known under a variety of names, such as the "Waterman's Knot" and the "Fisherman's Knot," this knot definitely seems of English origin, so the name English Knot or Englishman's Knot is an appropriate one.

The tie is an easy one, done thus: Lay the ends of two ropes — "A" and "B" —so that they overlap, each pointing opposite to the other (fig. 1). Tie the end of Rope A around the standing part of Rope B, using a simple Overhand Knot. Then tie the end of Rope B around the standing part of Rope A in identical fashion (fig. 2). Draw the standing parts in opposite directions and as the ends come together, the knots will jam into one, forming a strong join.

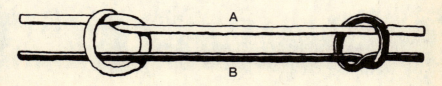

A

B

fig. 2

VI
LOOPS AND NOOSES

About Loops

Loops figure prominently in the early pages of this book, some of the knots discussed, specifically the Running Knot or Slip Knot, actually belong with those about to be described.

This chapter is limited to special loops of the most useful type, with other loop formations appearing later. It must be remembered that there are as many variations of loops as there are of knots.

In fact, the more complicated the formation, the more chance there is of going astray. Hence, it is preferable here to concentrate on basic formations.

The Bowline

This knot is also known as the "Standing Bowline." Though simple, it is somewhat tantalizing, and can be quickly and automatically made once you gain the knack.

There are several ways of making it, but one of the easiest is as follows: Start with an overhand loop, which serves as an "eye." Put end "A" (fig.1) up through the loop, then under the standing part, to form a turn (fig. 2).

This brings the end over the standing part. Thrust the end down through the "eye" to form a bight (fig. 3). Grip both portions of the bight with one hand and pull on the standing part with the other hand.

Thus the eye becomes a tight knot below which you have a large loop for mooring purposes or for lowering and raising persons or objects. The knot is strong and will neither slip nor jam.

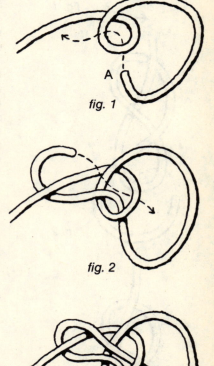

fig. 1

fig. 2

fig. 3

Figure Eight or False Bowline

Tie a Figure Eight Knot, starting upward with an overhand loop and following with an underhand loop above it. Allow enough rope for a long end, as you bring it down through the lower loop to complete the Figure Eight (fig. 1).

Form a bight below the knot and bring the rope end down through the lower loop of the Figure Eight (fig's 2 & 3), following the same line as before. Pull the knot tight and the job is done.

As you see, this resembles the familiar Standing Bowline. Some claim this is the "True Bowline," meaning it was the original Bowline or at least an early type.

Others call this the "False Bowline," and that is appropriate because it will give under too much strain. However, that can be remedied to some degree by adding a Half Hitch to the loose end, as shown (fig. 4). The knot, when tightened, will then tend to jam.

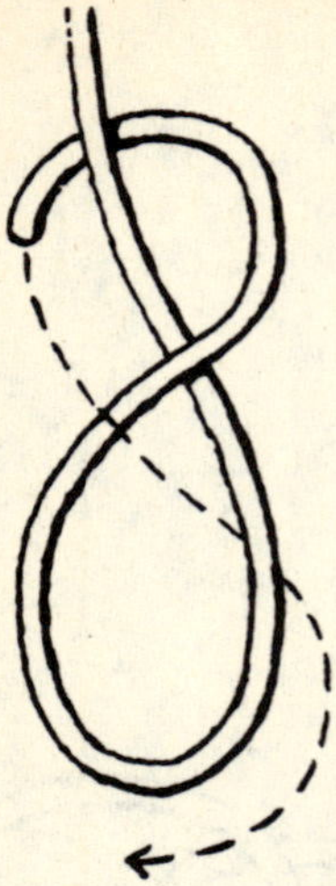

fig. 1

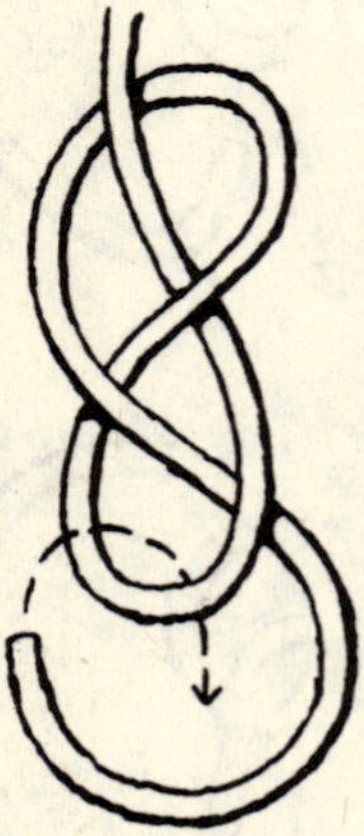

fig. 2

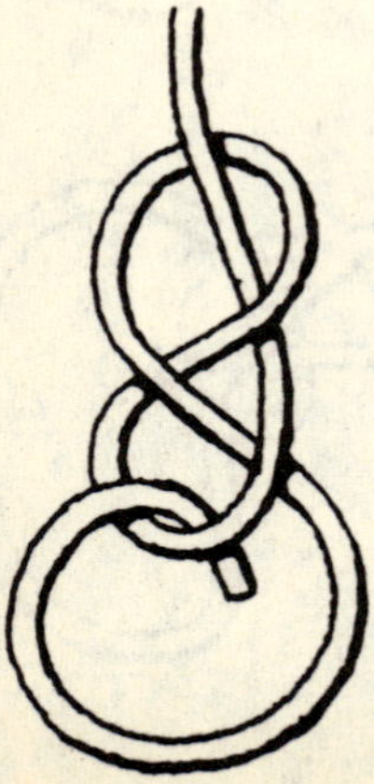

fig. 3

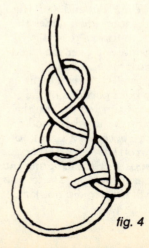

fig. 4

Spanish Bowline

There are various ways of forming this excellent Bowline featured by a double loop. The method shown here is one of the simplest.

Begin by doubling a bight under the center of rope, crossing the ends and forming two loops (fig. 1). Draw each strand up through the loop to form two extended bights as shown in figure 2.

Each bight must then be twisted in an outward direction. This is easily done by gripping them with the thumb and forefinger of each hand and turning them away from each other. A half twist puts them in position (fig. 3).

Now, take each side of the lower loop. Draw these upward so they pass over and then under the strands that compose the upper loops, exactly as shown by the arrows in figure 3.

Pull the center knot tight, retaining the loops in their extended fashion. This forms the two-looped Spanish Bowline (fig. 4). Inverted, it is gripped by the ends, so that the loops dangle and can be used for lifting purposes.

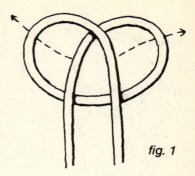

fig. 1

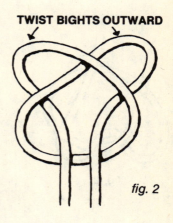

TWIST BIGHTS OUTWARD

fig. 2

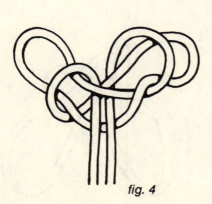

fig. 4

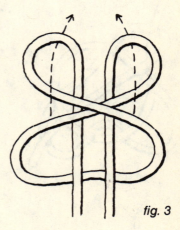

fig. 3

French Bowline

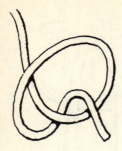

fig. 1

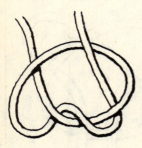

fig. 2

Here is a "double-loop" Bowline with a special advantage: When you draw out one loop, it tightens the other. This makes it useful as a double sling. You can sit in one loop, wrap the other around your chest and let your friends hoist you high, wide and handsome.

Start with a simple Overhand Knot as in figure 1. Then bring the end over again, forming what is virtually a Double Overhand (fig. 2). Now, run the end up through the loop, carry it around behind the standing part and bring it down through the same loop, in front (fig. 3).

Then, in a simple reversal of the course, bring the rope end back along its track. Tighten the knot thus formed and the French Bowline is complete (fig. 4). This knot is sometimes called the "Portuguese Bowline," but that name is also applied to another double formation.

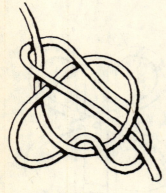

fig. 3

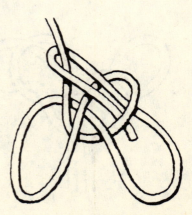

fig. 4

The Lasso or Honda Knot

To form a lasso, tie a tight Overhand Knot in the rope end to serve as a "stopper" (fig. 1). Then tie a loose Overhand Knot in the standing part, above the end, so that the end emerges from the front of the loop, toward the right (fig. 2).

Now, bring the end of the rope in back of the loop and draw it up through from the left (as shown by the arrow in fig. 2), to form a loop within the loop, the end going through the lower portion of the knot as shown in figure 3.

Though simple, this knot must be carefully formed, so that when it is drawn tight the "stopper" knot will catch and hold. This also is known as a "Honda Knot."

To complete the lariat, draw a bight through the large loop to form a running noose.

fig. 1

fig. 2

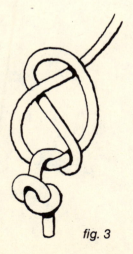

fig. 3

VII
ROPE SHORTENINGS

Too Much Rope

When you have too much rope for a particular purpose, there is a simple solution — shorten it.

Someone unfamiliar with rope work might think that means cutting the rope to the required length. But sometimes you don't know how much rope you require until you have experimented with it; or, you may not want to cut the rope. You may need it later as a full-length rope. So the problem is how to make it shorter but still keep it long.

That is done with "shortening" knots or other formations. These "shorteners" are not only useful, many of them are ornamental. Most rope workers are introduced to fancy rope work through knots of this type.

So try this "short" way to expert ropemanship with these shortening formations. You will find it intriguing, as well as practical. After experimenting with these, you can continue with more ornamental knots in the following chapter entitles "Fancy and Decorative Knots."

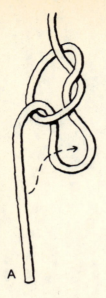

A

fig. 1

Single Chain Twist

Commonly known as a "Monkey Chain," this is a quick, easy and effective way of shortening rope. First you tie a Slip Knot around the end ("A"), allowing the end as much length as desired (fig. 1).

Then take a bight below the knot and push it down through the bight already formed there (fig. 2). That is, you put the bight through the bight, making them about equal size.

Continue thus, bight after bight, each through the one above until you have all the "links" that you require. Then push end "A" down through the final bight (fig. 3). That equalizes ends "A" and "B" — each going through a loop — and pulling the ends tightens the chain.

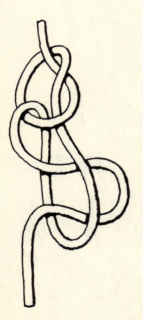

fig. 2

fig. 3

Double Chain Twist

Take two bights in a rope, one in each hand, so that it forms a letter "M," the end ("A") dangling at the left, the standing part ("B") at the right (fig. 1). Then cross the right-hand bight in front of the left to form a loop.

This gives you three strands of rope which may be termed "X," "Y," and "Z" from left to right (fig. 2). Starting downward from the crossing, bring "X" over in front of "Y," "Z" over in front of "X," "Y" over in front of "Z," and so on, moving the strands in left-right, left-right order (fig. 3).

As you do this, keep drawing end "A" completely through the loop, otherwise it will become snarled from the continued twisting. At the bottom, end "A" goes through the loop automatically (fig. 3). By drawing on ends "A" and "B" the double chain is tightened.

Due to the twisting process, the knots formed in this type of shortening are sometimes termed "Twist Knots."

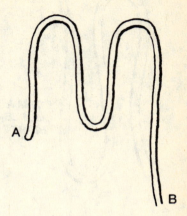

fig. 1

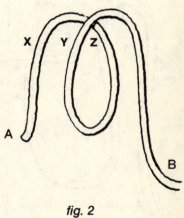

fig. 2

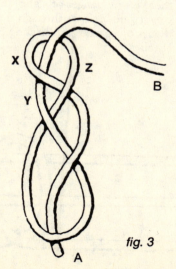

fig. 3

68

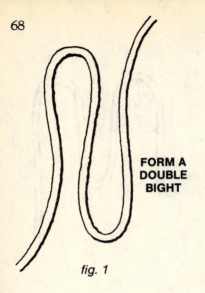

FORM A DOUBLE BIGHT

fig. 1

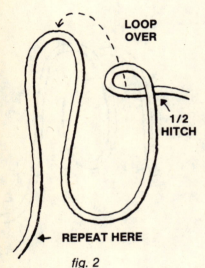

LOOP OVER

1/2 HITCH

← REPEAT HERE

fig. 2

The Sheepshank

The most famous and useful of rope "shorteners," this also is a "strengthener", as it supplies triple strands at any portion of a single rope.

Take a bight near the center of a rope and take another bight in the opposite direction, one running upward, the other downward (fig. 1). For simplicity, assume that the upward bight is at the left, the standing part of the rope at the right.

Twist the standing part to form an underhand loop and slip it over the upward bight, pulling the loop tight so that it is practically locked in place (fig. 2).

Now do the same with the downward bight, but in reverse fashion. To simplify this, turn the rope upside down so that you will be performing exactly the same operation as before.

The result is simplicity itself — two opposite bights in the center of the rope, each gripped by a Half Hitch (fig. 3). The harder you pull on the rope ends, the firmer it becomes. If there is any danger of a slip, insert two toggles or bars through the loops that project from the circling Half Hitches.

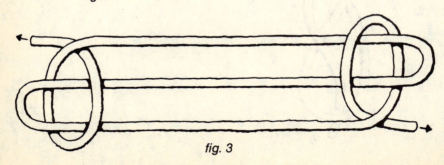

fig. 3

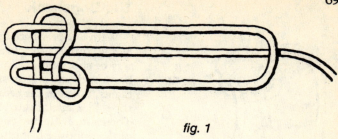

fig. 1

The Catshank

Similar to the Sheepshank in appearance and purpose, this also can be made in the center of a long rope without using the ends, which makes it very practical for specific purposes.

To form the Catshank, tie two Running Knots or simple Slip Knots a foot or more apart. Double the rope between them to form opposite bights as with the Sheepshank. Draw the bights through those opposite knots until the rope is suitably shortened (fig. 1). Then pull the knots tight by tugging the main portions of the rope toward the ends.

This final action gives an excellent idea of the strength and resistance of the Catshank.

fig. 2

The Dogshank

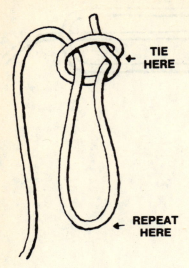

TIE HERE ←

← **REPEAT HERE**

fig. 1

With a rope where the ends are handy, this is a simple and effective way of shortening it still more. You begin with the customary opposite bights, taken in the center of the rope, like an elongated letter "S." Then simply tie one end to the bulge of the opposite bight, using a simple Overhand Knot (fig. 1). Tie the other end to its opposite bight in the same fashion. You can allow whatever length you want to the projecting ends, the actual shortening being done by the shank.

Overhand Knot with Sheepshank

This is the simplest and quickest of all rope shortenings, when using a rope with both ends available. Form a doubled bight in the center of the rope (in "S"-shape) and tie the triple strands in an ordinary Overhand Knot. Pull it tight by the projecting bows or loops (fig. 1).

When these loops are fairly long, you can add a Sheepshank by throwing a Half Hitch around each loop, just as if it were the center of a bight — which it is (fig. 3). In this case, since the ends of the rope are accessible, you can make the hitches close to the loop ends. Then draw the rope ends right through the tiny loops thus formed and pull them tight (as shown by the arrows in fig. 3), jamming the hitches and giving them added strength. This can be done with an ordinary Sheepshank or Catshank, too, when the loose ends are handy.

Overhand Knot with Sheepshank

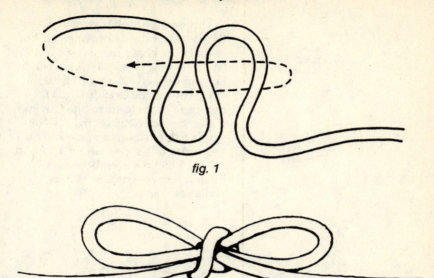

fig. 1

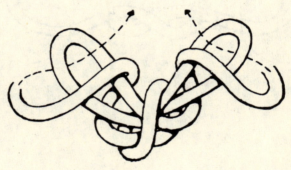

fig. 2

fig. 3

fig. 4

Jury Knot with Sheepshank

This combination is strong and useful, as well as highly ornamental. You begin by making a Jury Mast Knot (see following chapter), which winds up with opposite loops or bights, along with single strands (fig. 1). Use the single ropes to form Sheepshanks with the proper bights (fig. 2). The whole combination can be made in the center of a rope without access to the ends and the knot between the hitches relieves strain as well as adding strength.

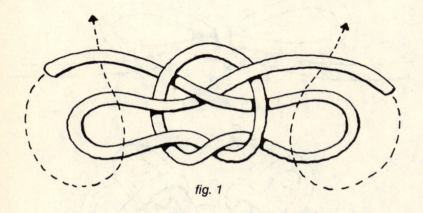

fig. 1

fig. 2

VIII
FANCY AND DECORATIVE KNOTS

Plain and Fancy

From plain knots fancier types can be formed, since the basic features of bights, loops, and turns are merely compounded in the making of the more intricate rope designs.

A knot that is complicated is not entitled to the rating of "fancy." It should be decorative as well — and if useful, so much the better. Along with these features, there is the actual formation of the knots, some having special merit because of the ingenious ways in which they are fashioned.

These points will become apparent when working with the knots in this section.

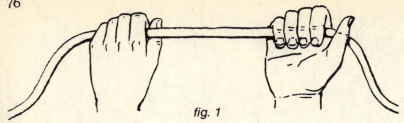

fig. 1

Tom Fool Knot

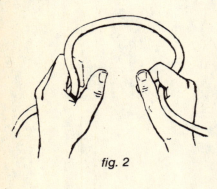

fig. 2

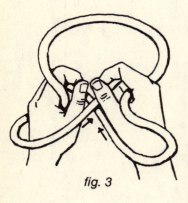

fig. 3

This is simply an extension of the Running Knot, a double form which may be made very rapidly in three moves, as follows: Grip the rope in the left fist, knuckles down, and in the right fist, knuckles up, allowing several inches of rope between them (fig. 1). Turn the hands toward each other (fig. 2), bringing the knuckles together, at the same time slanting them slightly forward and downward, so that the in-between rope forms a bight extending out beyond the fists (fig. 3).

With the first two fingers of the right hand, clip the rope extending in back of the left; with the first two fingers of the left hand, clip the rope extending in back of the right hand. Draw the hands apart (fig. 4).

The final action forms the double loop. This is a type of handcuff tie, as the loops can be slipped over a person's wrists and then drawn tight, though it needs added knots to make it secure.

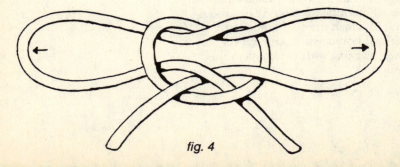

fig. 4

The Shamrock

A highly ornamental knot, yet easily formed if the rope is laid out on a flat surface and the directions are carefully followed. You need a short rope since both ends are used in the formation of the Shamrock.

Tie a simple Overhand Knot with the loop above it and bring the ends up and above the loop, one on each side (fig. 1). The end at the right ("A") is then carried toward the left and the loop is extended to lie across it. The end at the left ("B") is then laid across the loop toward the right (fig. 2).

Carry end "A" down over both portions of the bight formed by end "B." Push end "A" down through the left half of the original Overhand Knot (as shown by the arrow in fig. 2), through the little loop "X".

Now bring end "B" down beneath both portions of the bight formed by end "A." That done, work end "B" up through the tiny loop forming the right half of the original Overhand Knot, indicated as "Y" (as shown by the arrow in fig. 2).

Pull the ends ("A" and "B") straight down, tightening the center of the Shamrock and at the same time arranging the three big loops in uniform fashion to form the petals of the design (fig. 3).

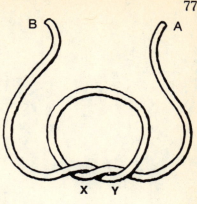

fig. 1

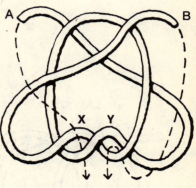

fig. 2

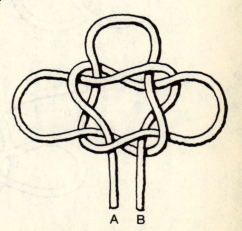

fig. 3

Jury Mast Knot

Working from left to right, form an overhand loop ("X") with the left hand. Continue and form another overhand loop ("Y") with the right hand. Hold these so that the left loop ("X") slightly overlaps the right loop (fig. 1).

Let these loops lie loosely on the hands which are palms up, fingers tip to tip. Dip the left thumb and forefinger down through "X" and grip the left side of "Y." Work the right thumb and forefinger up through "Y" and grip the right side of "X" (as shown by the arrows in fig. 1). Pull the hands apart and the knot is formed (fig. 2).

It gains its name from the fact that it was used to rig a temporary "jury" mast, the center being placed over the top of the mast and the loops fixed with guy lines to the deck.

LAYOUT

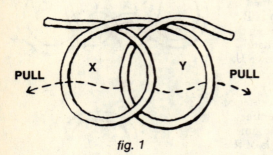

PULL   X   Y   PULL

fig. 1

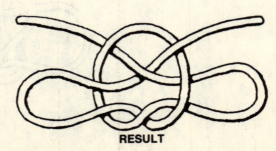

RESULT

fig. 2

Double Jury Knot

Here you lay out three overhand loops ("X," "Y," "Z"), in that order from left to right. "Y" overlaps "X" and "Z" overlaps "Y," as shown in figure 1.

The loops should be placed on a flat surface, so that they can be easily handled. Draw the right side of loop "X" over the first rope to its right, under the next and over the last.

At the same time, work the left side of loop "Z" under the first rope to its left —which is the right side of "X" — then over the next and under the last (as shown by the arrows in fig. 1). Pull those extended ropes toward left and right and you will have two big loops (fig. 2).

Those account for "X" and "Z," but what about the middle loop, "Y"? You can reclaim "Y" by drawing it out from the bottom of the knot, so that it forms a third loop below and between the other two (fig. 2).

For nautical purposes, a fourth loop can be formed by knotting the two loose ends, but when used to attach a guy line, these are generally spliced for greater holding strength.

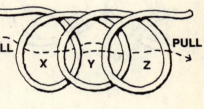

fig. 1

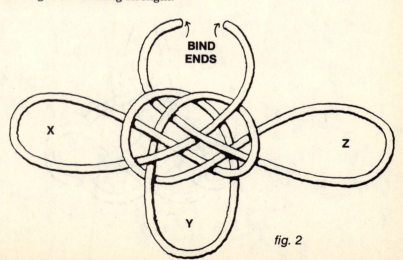

fig. 2

An Oriental Knot

Typical of many knots of Oriental origin, this one is formed by weaving the rope ends through three loops, in an alternating "overhand" manner.

Start with a loop in the center of the rope and form two others to the left side and below it, one overhand, the other underhand, as shown in figure 1.

Cross the rope ends right over left (fig. 2) up through the lower loops, the left end going under and over, the right end over and under (as indicated by the arrows in fig. 2).

Weave the ends on up through the top loop, the left going under the loop, over the right end and under the loop; the right going over the loop, under the left end and over the loop (fig. 3).

If the ends are tied or drawn up together, the knotted center may be tightened, so that the lower loops resemble those of a Double Bowline. Or the ends can be seized to form a third loop, like the Jury Mast Knot or similar designs.

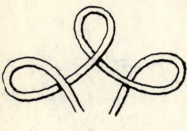

fig. 1

fig. 2

fig. 3

IX
TRICKS WITH KNOTS

Here we have a series of really baffling rope tricks, which the reader will find easy to perform once he "knows his knots." The reason the knot tricks are "easy" is that knots, loops and other formations are very difficult for the eye to follow. No quickness of the hand is needed to deceive the eye in this type of wizardry. The ropes accomplish the deception.

For that reason most knot tricks should be done slowly and deliberately; but at the same time smoothly. That is, they should be practiced to the point where there is no hesitation, for any fumbling may give away some important maneuver that is being done at that particular point.

Hasty work, hesitation, or anything that detracts from smoothness gives the impression that the trick is all in the knots, rather than the performer's skill. Actually, that is true, but it is the one thing that the rope wizard doesn't want his audience to discover.

Once you have learned your knot tricks, you can concentrate on them when you demonstrate them. You don't have to "sell" your audience with glib talk, nor worry about sleight-of-hand, special gimmicks, or other problems that confront the impromptu or amateur magician. Knot tricks are "self-working" in the true sense of the term.

Most knot tricks are good "repeaters," too. The sort that can be worked time and again before the same group of spectators and still keep them puzzled.

It is better, though, to vary your tricks, expanding your "repertoire" as far as possible so that it will retain an air of novelty.

FINGER TRAPPED

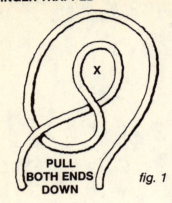

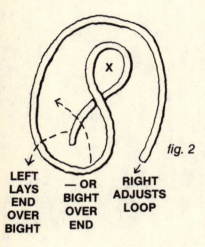

PULL
BOTH ENDS
DOWN

fig. 1

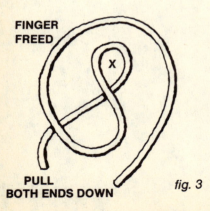

LEFT
LAYS
END
OVER
BIGHT

— OR
BIGHT
OVER
END

RIGHT
ADJUSTS
LOOP

fig. 2

FINGER
FREED

PULL
BOTH ENDS DOWN

fig. 3

Slip the Loop

A short rope is laid on the table so that it forms a figure eight with one end completely encircling it (fig. 1). Have a friend place his finger in the center loop — the upper circle of the "8" — and you pull the ends of the rope. His finger is trapped in a tightened double loop.

When you insert your own finger, however, the result is different. A tug of the ends and the loop whisks completely clear. In brief, the loop can either trap the finger or come clear, whichever way you choose.

The trick depends on how you lay the rope. Set it as shown in the first diagram and you will snare the finger when it is placed in the loop. Lay the rope as shown in the second drawing and it will come clear.

In laying the rope, start with the left end and carry the right end down below the left, so it forms an open bight instead of a closed loop. Then continue clear around with the right end. This is shown in the third diagram, which is the crux of the trick because: As the right hand draws its end tighter, the left hand completes the lower loop by simply laying its end over the bight to produce the "finger trap" shown in the first diagram. Or, instead, the left hand simply lifts the bight and lays it over the loose end, forming the second setup, wherein the loops slide free.

In either case, the slight action of the left hand goes unnoticed as it is apparently adjusting the rope. To all appearances, the figures are identical.

On Again — Off Again

Here is another version of the finger and loop stunt, which uses a different way of placing the cord. Again, it appears in the shape of an "8," but the upper loop, in which the finger is inserted, may be made considerably larger (fig. 1).

Arranged as in the first diagram, the loop will snag the finger when the ends of the cord are pulled. The second diagram shows the form in which the loops pull clear.

Start with the left end, forming the loops as in the "key" diagram, so that the end can be slid over or under the bight to produce the result desired (fig. 2).

This is recommended as an alternate for the previous method. Switch from one to the other and you will keep keen observers baffled when you repeat the stunt.

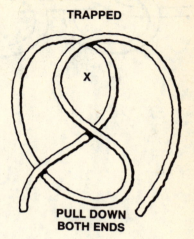

TRAPPED

**PULL DOWN
BOTH ENDS**

fig. 1

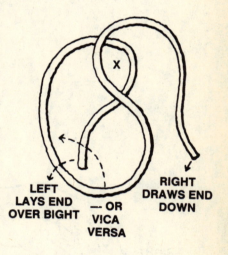

**LEFT
LAYS END
OVER BIGHT**

**— OR
VICA
VERSA**

**RIGHT
DRAWS END
DOWN**

fig. 2

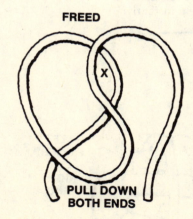

FREED

**PULL DOWN
BOTH ENDS**

fig. 3

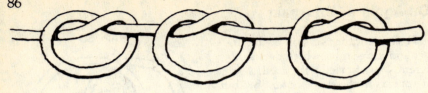

fig. 1

Go-Go Knots

You tie a series of simple Overhand Knots along a length of rope, working from the left end to the right, so that the knots run in regular order (fig. 1). Taking the ends of the rope, you say "Go!", give the rope a quick stretch and the knots are gone.

This is done as follows: Keep the knots "open" so they can be looped or gathered over the extended left fingers, starting with the knot at the left. The right hand helps in this procedure and you must be careful to place each knot exactly the same way, without twisting the rope. The right hand tucks its end of the rope between the projecting left fingers. Turn the left hand so the right can grip the left end of the rope (fig. 2). With the word "Go!", pull the hands wide apart. The left hand comes through the coiled knots, eliminating them instantly.

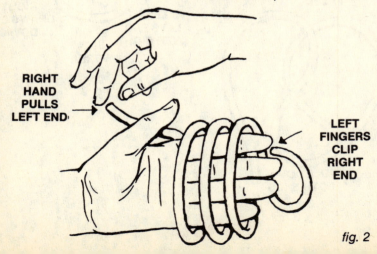

RIGHT
HAND
PULLS
LEFT END

LEFT
FINGERS
CLIP
RIGHT
END

fig. 2

Shake Them Away

This is a more deliberate version of the "Go-Go Knots," done in one-hand style. The right hand makes a hypnotic pass as the left hand shakes the rope and the knots evaporate.

The trick is done as follows: Proceed as with the "Go-Go Knots" until the left fingers obtain their hold on the right end of the rope. Then turn the left hand completely over, so it is knuckles downward. Let the coils slide from the hand as you shake the rope and the trick is done.

Again, be sure that the knots are not drawn too tightly, as they must shake away easily. This has a very mysterious effect.

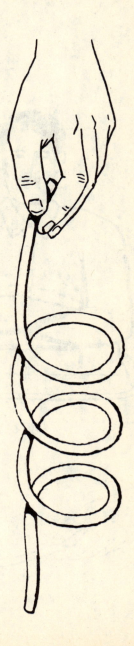

The Impossible Knot

Most people would agree it's impossible to tie a knot in the middle of a rope while you are holding both ends. So you take a rope and proceed to prove that you can do it.

Here is the method: Lay a short rope on a table and fold your arms (fig. 1). Foreword and grip one end of the rope with the thumb and fingers of your right hand, the other with your left. Simply unfold your arms and draw the ends of the rope apart. As your arms unfold, a knot will tie itself automatically (fig. 2).

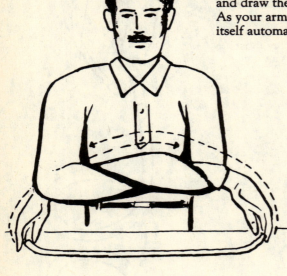

fig. 1

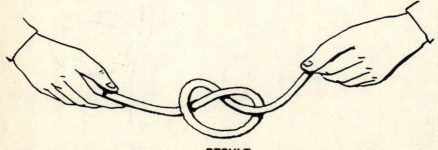

RESULT

fig. 2

Double Cut and Restored Rope

In this simple but effective version of the "cut rope" trick, you cut a rope into three lengths which are then knotted together. A few magic passes, and the knots are gone and the single rope is restored in full.

Actually, you don't cut the rope into three lengths at all. You begin by showing a single rope, then double it into two bights up and down (fig. 1), so that you can tie the ends to the bights in the manner of a Catshank (fig. 2).

Draw out the loops to equal lengths, so that only an inch (or less) of rope projects from each end. State that you have divided the rope into three sections —which you have — and that you will now cut the sections apart. To all appearances, you do just that, but in actuality you don't.

Instead of cutting the bights, you use a pair of scissors to cut the standing part of each rope, just below the knot (see fig. 2). That is, you really cut off the rope ends and the knots with them, but the knots naturally stay in place.

You now take the rope by its new "ends" and the two knots, spaced equally along the rope, give the false impression that the rope has been cut into three parts, whereas it is still all one.

To "restore" the rope: Take one end on the left hand. With the right hand, slowly coil the rope around the left, drawing the right hand down the rope as you do. As you come to the knots, carry them along with the right hand, which takes them off the end.

You must now dispose of the telltale knots. The simplest way is to reach for the scissors which you used to cut the rope. Pick them up from

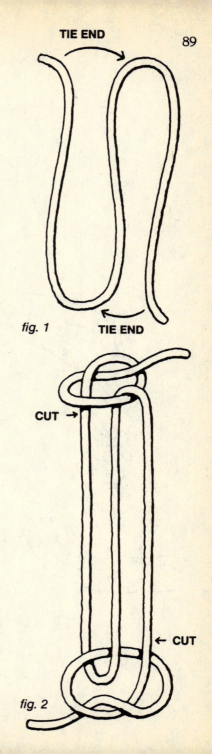

TIE END

fig. 1

TIE END

CUT →

← CUT

fig. 2

the table with the right hand, leaving the knots in their place. Wave the scissors, saying that they cut the rope and will now magically restore it — along with the secret words "Mumbo Jumbo." Lay aside the scissors, take the ends of the rope and stretch it straight, showing it "restored."

Comedy "Cut-Rope" Climax

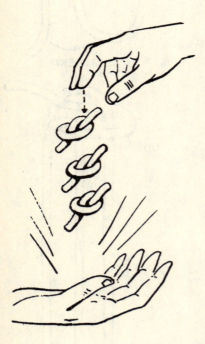

Disposal of the cut-off knots is the only problem with the "Double Cut" rope trick. It's not much of a problem, if you have some article lying on the table to hide them, such as a handkerchief which can later be pocketed, along with the knots. However, there is a simpler solution to the problem; that is to let the knots dispose of themselves, as part of a comedy climax. In this case, you don't bother to coil the rope around your left hand. You give the ends to someone and tell him to hold the rope taut.

Then you turn to another person and ask, "Are you sure those are knots?" When he says, "Yes," you announce: "All right, I'll restore the rope by magic" — here you make some mystic passes — "and since we won't need the knots, you can have them."

With that, you pluck the knots from the rope and hand them to your friend, while you take the rope and show it intact. Oddly enough, this bold handling of the knots makes the trick all the more puzzling to some people.

Snap-Off Knots

Another climax to the "Double Cut" is to retain the rope yourself after you have made the cuts. Dangle it by the ends, repeat the magic words and give the rope a hard snap by spreading your arms and pulling it taut.

The knots will then snap off the rope and fall to the floor while the onlookers stare in surprise at the restored rope, the whole effect being instantaneous. You can give the rope for inspection and then pick up the loose ends — or ignore them.

If you use this climax, be sure to cut the knots very close, so that they will snap away. With some types of rope, it also is a good plan to press them with thumb and fingers to make sure they are loose enough to snap off.

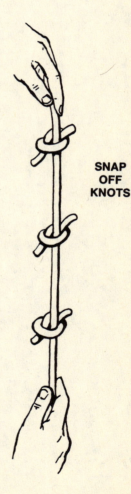

**SNAP
OFF
KNOTS**

X

ROPE TIES AND RELEASES

Sketches of Houdini coiling the rope for the "Amazing Knots" trick during the opening of a rope ties act.

Special Rope Stunts

Though the added effects in this chapter are simple to perform, they are somewhat different from ordinary knot tricks, and so have been included in a group of their own.

With these you require some emphasis on presentation, as some are performed "under cover" or require special appliances. Reserve them for the right audience or suitable occasion where they will be most effective.

Three Amazing Knots

You hold a six-foot length of rope between your hands, casually coil it, and give it a hard fling, retaining one end as you do so. Instantly, three knots appear at intervals along the rope!

These "Spirit Knots," as they are sometimes called, are secretly formed as follows:

Lay the left end of the rope across the open left hand, which is palm up. Bring the right hand palm up beneath the rope, grip the rope loosely and

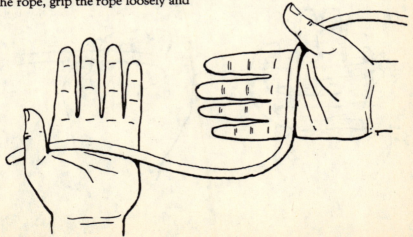

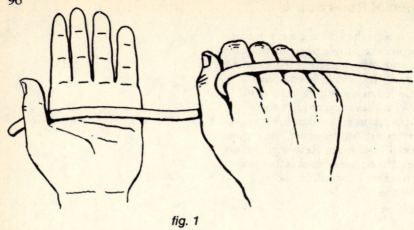

fig. 1

turn the right toward the left, so that the right comes knuckles down (fig. 1). This automatically forms an underhand loop, which the right hand hangs over the extended left fingers (fig. 2). Move the right hand along the rope to the right and repeat the maneuver with the second loop. Then go farther to the right and form a third loop the same way.

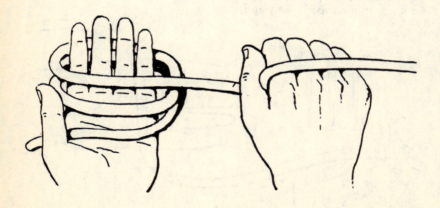

fig. 2

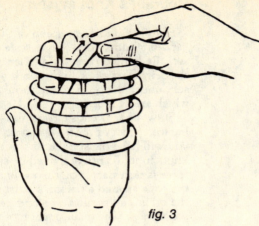

fig. 3

All this is done openly and above-
board. Now comes the simple but
unnoticed move that produces the
climax. As your right hand places the
final loop, you dip the right thumb
and forefinger through all three loops
and grip the left end of the rope (fig. 3).

Bring that end back through the
loops, draw it clear, and give the rope
a fling with the right hand, retaining
the end which you have gripped (fig. 4).

That action will form the knots
along the rope. Don't be stingy with
the loops; make them ample and the
trick is sure.

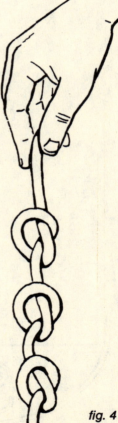

fig. 4

Houdini's Knot Mystery

Here is Houdini's version of the "spooky knots" on a larger scale, that actually baffled persons familiar with the original trick. You can do it yourself, under the proper conditions, which are as follows:

Show your friends a rope measuring thirty feet or more — and say that you will have the spooks tie some knots in it. To prove that some such force is necessary, you tie one end of the rope around a person's waist and the other end around a second person's waist. The main portion of the rope is lying coiled on the floor between your two volunteers (fig. 1). It is impossible to get at the rope and tie knots in it; that is, impossible for anyone except the friendly "spirits" upon whom you call. Since spirits work only in the dark, the lights are turned off.

You then tell the two volunteers to move to opposite corners of the room so the spooks will have space in which they can operate. You call for lights and "mysteriously" the rope is stretched taut between the two

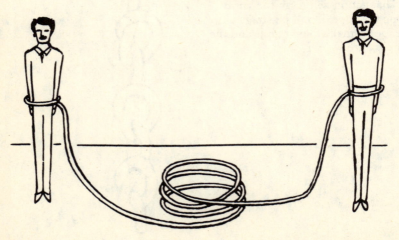

fig. 1

helpers with knots at regular intervals. Since you couldn't have had a thing to do with it, the knots must have been tied by the obliging spooks.

That, at least, is your story. Here is how you really do it. In coiling the rope on the floor use "underhand" loops as described in "Three Amazing Knots." But in this case, the loops must be very large, three feet across or more.

Once the lights are out, pick up all the loops together and drop them over the head and shoulders of the helper on the left (fig. 2). Start that person to the far corner of the room. That will draw out the rope and form the knots automatically (fig. 3), because *putting the loops over the helper is the same as putting the left end of the rope through the loops.* The end goes through the loops and the knots appear, but on a bigger scale and under mysterious conditions.

Just pick the proper helper for the person on the left; either a friend who will work with you, or someone who will blame the "spooks" for pushing them around. Then the trick will be all the simpler.

fig. 2

fig. 3

Knot Dissolving Tube

Here is something really fourth-dimensional. A fantastic tube that dissolves knots inserted into it!

To prove the tube's special properties, you take a light rope and tie a simple Overhand Knot around the outside of the tube, in such a manner that the left end ("A") is the upper end, and the right end ("B") is the lower end (fig. 1).

Bring the right strand of the rope a few inches downward, hold it against the tube with the left thumb while you carry the right end of the rope clear around the tube with the right hand. You then tie another knot, just like the first, using end "B" in the process.

Bring the right end downward again, and hold the rope with the left thumb while the right hand carries its end ("B") around the tube and ties a third knot. This is near the lower end of the tube and the rope end ("B") now dangles free (fig. 2).

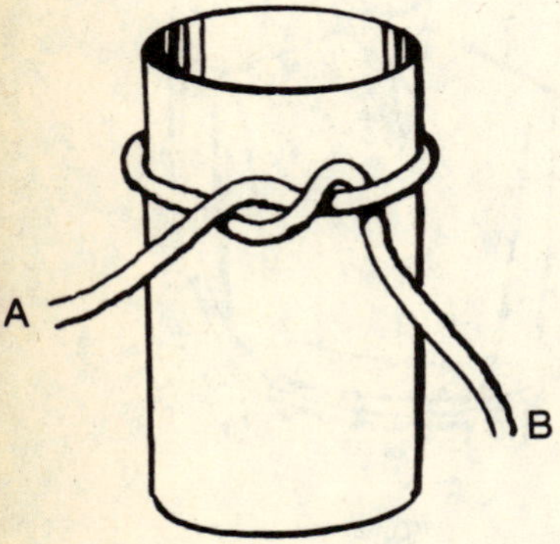

fig. 1

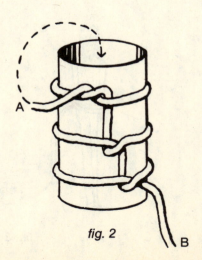

fig. 2

Now take the upper end of the rope ("A") and drop it down through the tube (as indicated by the arrow in fig. 2). When it comes out the bottom, give it to someone to hold.

Next, draw all the knots upward in a bunch and as they come off the top, push them down into the tube, stating that the dissolving process is ready to begin. Promptly take the free end of the rope ("B") and give it to someone else to hold.

Obviously, the knots are safely and soundly in the tube, but when the people pull the ends of the rope and you run the tube back and forth, they find to their amazement that the knots are gone (fig. 3). Tube and rope may then be examined.

This trick works if you follow instructions to the letter. You actually untie the knots when you drop the upper end down through the tube, but you have to stuff the knots in with it to complete the job.

This can be done with string as well as rope and any cardboard tube will do. Just make sure the cord is long enough, and the more mysterious or pseudo-scientific talk you add, the more impressive it will be.

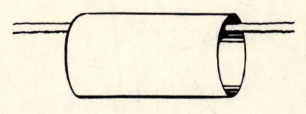

fig. 3

Rings and Loops

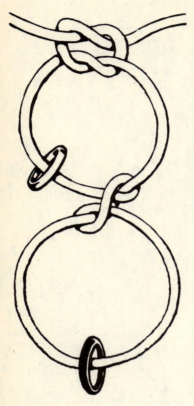

A stiff cord is used in this stunt, along with two rings or disks that should be quite different in appearance — say one black and one white. The rings have holes in the center and can be cut from heavy cardboard if metal rings are not handy.

The black ring is threaded on the cord, which is tied with a hard, firm knot, so as to form a loop some three or four inches in diameter, from which the black ring dangles. The white ring is then slid over one end of the cord, which is tied to form an upper loop of about the same size (fig. 1).

Three or four more knots are added at the top to make it all the more secure. Two persons hold the extended ends of the cord and a large handkerchief is thrown over the hanging loops and rings (fig. 2).

Now, you announce you will make the rings change places despite the solid knot that intervenes. You show

fig. 1

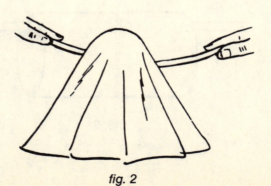

fig. 2

Now take the upper end of the rope ("A") and drop it down through the tube (as indicated by the arrow in fig. 2). When it comes out the bottom, give it to someone to hold.

Next, draw all the knots upward in a bunch and as they come off the top, push them down into the tube, stating that the dissolving process is ready to begin. Promptly take the free end of the rope ("B") and give it to someone else to hold.

Obviously, the knots are safely and soundly in the tube, but when the people pull the ends of the rope and you run the tube back and forth, they find to their amazement that the knots are gone (fig. 3). Tube and rope may then be examined.

This trick works if you follow instructions to the letter. You actually untie the knots when you drop the upper end down through the tube, but you have to stuff the knots in with it to complete the job.

This can be done with string as well as rope and any cardboard tube will do. Just make sure the cord is long enough, and the more mysterious or pseudo-scientific talk you add, the more impressive it will be.

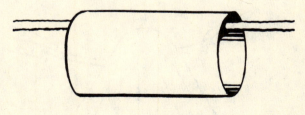

fig. 3

Rings and Loops

A stiff cord is used in this stunt, along with two rings or disks that should be quite different in appearance — say one black and one white. The rings have holes in the center and can be cut from heavy cardboard if metal rings are not handy.

The black ring is threaded on the cord, which is tied with a hard, firm knot, so as to form a loop some three or four inches in diameter, from which the black ring dangles. The white ring is then slid over one end of the cord, which is tied to form an upper loop of about the same size (fig. 1).

Three or four more knots are added at the top to make it all the more secure. Two persons hold the extended ends of the cord and a large handkerchief is thrown over the hanging loops and rings (fig. 2).

Now, you announce you will make the rings change places despite the solid knot that intervenes. You show

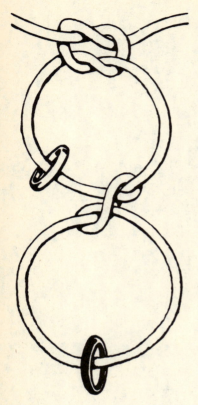

fig. 1

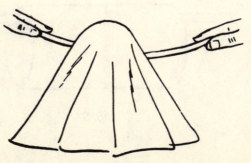

fig. 2

the positions of the rings, cover them again and work beneath the cloth for a few moments. When the handkerchief is removed, the rings have indeed changed places! To everyones amazement, the white ring is now on the lower loop and the black ring on the upper loop; but the knot between them is intact. In fact, the knots have to be untied to remove the rings from the cord.

Despite its seeming impossibility, the trick is subtly simple. Underneath the cloth, you grasp the loops on each side of the center knot and push them toward each other. Thanks to the stiff cord, the knot loosens and you can run the upper ring along the cord and through the knot, down to the lower loop (as shown by the arrows in fig. 3).

Reverse the process with the other ring, bringing it up through the loosened knot to the upper loop. Then pull the knot tight again, good and tight, so no one will realize how you worked the trick. With a little practice, this can all be done quite rapidly.

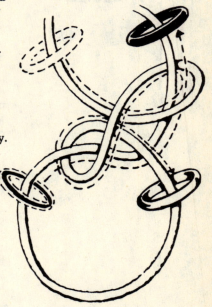

fig. 3

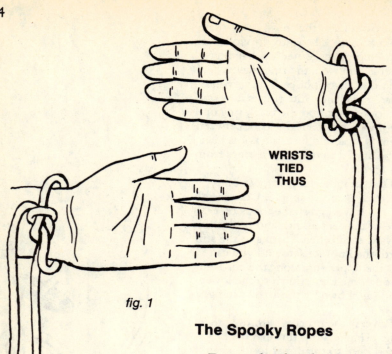

**WRISTS
TIED
THUS**

fig. 1

The Spooky Ropes

Two six-foot lengths of rope are used in this surprising stunt, wherein you call on "spooks" to aid you in producing otherwise impossible results. One rope is tied about your left wrist and the other about the right, each wrist being tied in the center of its respective rope (fig. 1).

This leaves two ends dangling from each rope. You sit down in a chair, *cross* your arms (fig. 2) and let people draw the ends of the ropes around in back of you, tying them together behind you and fixing them to the back of the chair so that your arms are literally clamped across your chest (fig. 3).

Now, some objects are placed in front of you on a table, such as a pad and pencil, an alarm clock, a rubber balloon, a small glass of water. A screen or cloth is raised to hide you from the spectators, or they step into another room and close the door. Immediately, spooky things happen.

The alarm clock starts to ring, the balloon explodes with a bang. You finally call for people to remove the screen or return to the room. When they do, they find you tied as tightly as ever. But the balloon is burst, the alarm clock is still ringing, the water is gone from the glass and there is a message written on the pad: "We were here — The Spooks."

You now have people cut or untie the ropes to make sure that they are knotted as tightly as originally, which makes everything all the more baffling, as it seems impossible that you could have done the spooky work without releasing yourself from the chair. Yet that is precisely what you do. Or at least partially, as the knots are never untied.

The moment you are alone, slide down in the chair, twist to the left and slide your upper arm, the right, over your head so that you can come clear (fig. 4), like skinning away a tight fitting sweater. You turn about completely in the process.

Though your wrists are still tied, you now have enough slack to reach the table, where you write the message, blow up the balloon and drink the water. You start the alarm clock ringing, burst the balloon with the pencil point and reverse your procedure with the ropes, twisting yourself back up in the chair while pulling your right arm down over your head again.

ARMS CROSSED THUS

fig. 2

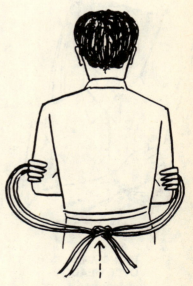

ROPES TIED IN REAR

fig. 3

That's how they find you, all tied up as you were at the start. You can even let them apply sealing wax to the knots to prove you have not tampered with them. This not only adds to the mystery, it serves as a reason why they must cut the ropes or work the knots loose afterward.

Everyone is likely to believe that you got out of the ropes and somehow tied yourself back in them, which is all the more wonderful — or would be if you could do it!

One final point: *never fold your arms* when working this trick or you will be boxed for sure. Simply *cross* them so that the right lies over the left; then you can always wriggle out, even when the ropes are pulled very tight.

But if some skeptic wants to try the trick himself or argues that you weren't securely bound, put him in the chair and tie him. First, however, get him to fold his arms, or draw the ropes up through as if they were folded. He just won't get out.

**BRING ARM
OVER HEAD**

fig. 4

Quickie Spook Trick

Here is a simplified version of the "Spooky Ropes" which is quick and easy. You are tied as in the previous trick, arms crossed and wrist ropes brought around in back of you and knotted to a chair.

Things then happen in the same swift, uncanny fashion. But in this case you don't have to wriggle partly free, the trick is done at the very start.

After each wrist has been tied, you let the ropes dangle, explaining how you intend to have them tied behind your back. As you talk, bring your hands palm to palm, but with fingers pointing in opposite direction. The middle fingers of the right hand clip the ropes dangling from the left wrist. The left hand fingers catch the ropes that hang from the right wrist, in the same fashion (fig. 1). Rapidly fold your arms, turning your palms toward your body, running the ropes between your fingers as you do.

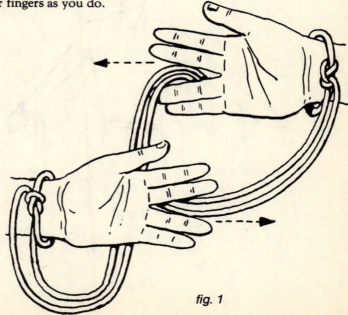

fig. 1

Boldly, but smoothly, you are actually reversing the direction of the ropes, so that they double back on themselves. Nobody sees this, because your wrists hide the knots. People suppose that the ropes run the proper way, so you seem to be securely tied. All you have to do is spread your arms wide apart and you can reach and handle the objects on the table.

Afterward, you clamp your arms together as though they were firmly bound as everyone thinks. In this case, have the ropes cut at the back when the trick is over, so you can spread your arms and let the ropes dangle before asking anyone to release your wrists (fig. 2). This kills any clue to the reversal of the ropes.

fig. 2

XI
SPECIAL TRICKS

String and Scissors

Two hundred years ago, the cheva-
lier Pinetti astounded Paris by escap-
ing from a doubled chain, looped
through metal rings attached to his
legs and locked to a post. The feat
was explained by a writer named
Decremps, as shown in the following
pages.

Figure 1 shows the chains before
the escape, which was performed
inside a cabinet. Figure 2 explains
how the escape was accomplished.
Figure 3 demonstrates the principle
behind the escape with a looped
string and a pair of scissors: draw the
loop through one handle and then the
other, and then spread the loop over
the points of the scissors.

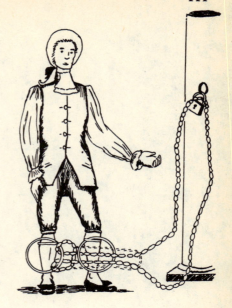

fig. 1

fig. 3

fig. 2

The Disentangled Scissors

More than 50 years later, a writer named Cramer supplied a more detailed version of the String and Scissors trick, called "The Disentangled Scissors,"in his book The Secret Out. People have been doing the trick ever since.

This is an old but capital trick. A piece of string is fastened to the scissors, as shown, and both the ends of the cord are held by the hand or tied firmly to a post or other immovable object (fig. 1).

To remove the scissors from the cord, take the loop end of the string and pass it through the upper handle as shown by the dotted line. Let the loop be carried still further towards the lower handle, until it is passed complete around the scissors (fig. 2), you then can remove them, as the string will slip easily through the handles.

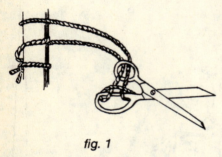

fig. 1

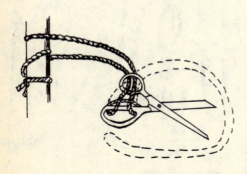

fig. 2

Ropes through Coat

Hold two long ropes side by side
and push the ends through one sleeve
of a coat and out the other (fig. 1).
Give one end of each rope to one person, and the other ends to another
(fig. 2). When they pull the ropes
hard, the coat falls to the ground
(fig. 3).

The secret is the two ropes originally shown are not single ropes.
They are each doubled in the center,
and their centers bound together with
thread (fig. 4). This joint is covered
while you run the "two ropes"
through the sleeves. When the two
people pull hard enough, the thread
breaks and the coat falls to the
ground.

fig. 1

fig. 2

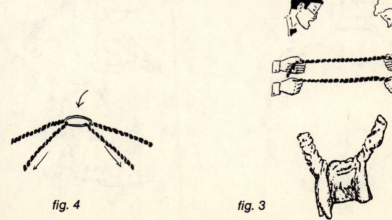

fig. 4

fig. 3

Ring on a String

Give someone a large flexible ring, then allow your wrists to be loosely tied with a length of rope between them (fig. 1). Take the ring, then turn your back for a few moments (fig. 2). Turn back around and show how the rung is now on the string (fig. 3). To accomplish this, work the ring under one wrist loop and over the hand onto the string (fig. 4). Use a ring from a vacuum cleaner or a jar.

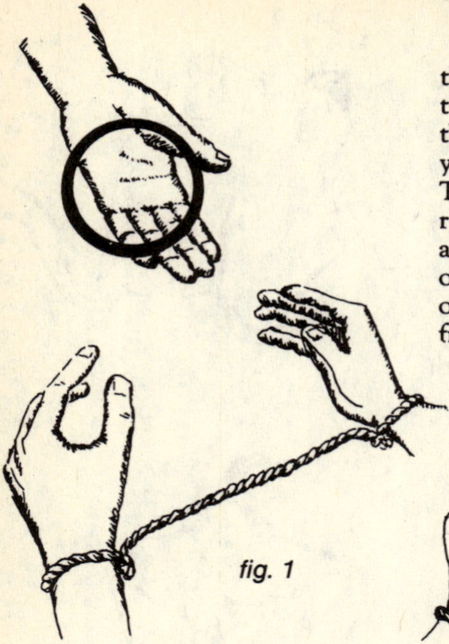

fig. 1

fig. 3

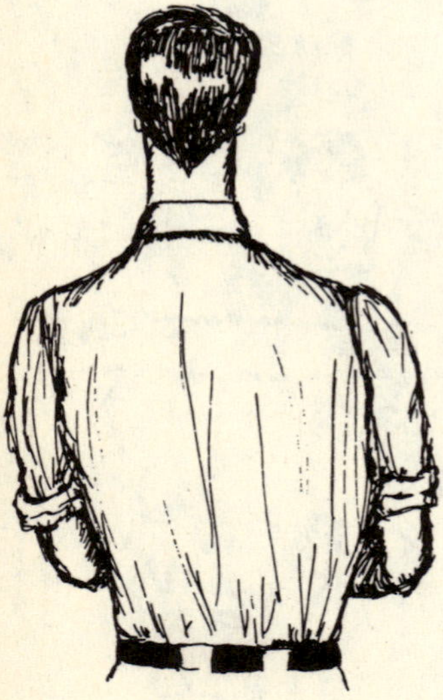

fig. 2

fig. 4

String through the Buttonhole

A loop of string is passed through a buttonhole, and held by the thumb. The thumb and one finger of each hand are then slipped through the loops on the opposite sides. The hands are suddenly drawn apart and the string comes right out of the buttonhole, apparently through the cloth of the coat.

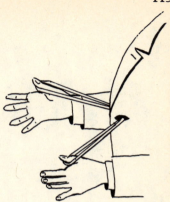

fig. 1

This is done as follows: Push the loop through the buttonhole, and hold it with a thumb in each end loop (fig. 1). Swing the right hand over towards the left, and hook the right little finger in either one of the strings that run from the left thumb to the buttonhole. Then bring the left hand toward the right, and hook the left little finger in one of the strings running from the right hand. The loop will now be held as shown in figure 2, which is the key to the whole trick. The string seems to be firmly through the buttonhole, but it can be drawn free in an instant.

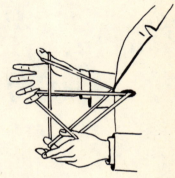

fig. 2

Release the string with the little finger of one hand, and the thumb of the other hand. Then draw the hands rapidly apart. The string will come clear of the buttonhole, and will still be between the hands (fig. 3). In the drawing, the string has been released by the left little finger and the right thumb.

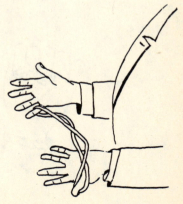

fig. 3

Knot the Rope

Here is another seemingly impossible trick — to tie a knot in the middle of a rope with both ends tied around your wrists!

The trick requires a light rope at least 3 feet long. Have someone tie the ends around your wrists, with a length of rope between then. Then proceed as follows: Turn your back, take a loop of the rope between the wrists and force it up under the band encircling the left wrist. Give this loop a twist and pass it over the hand (fig. 1), down the wrist, and back under the band again. A knot will appear on the rope between the wrists (fig. 2).

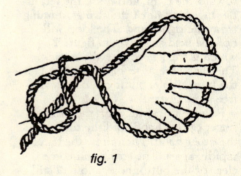

fig. 1

fig. 2

The Knotless Knot

Hold a handkerchief as shown in Fig. 1. Bring the right end ("A") under, behind, and over the left wrist, and push it through the loop, as indicated by the arrow in figure 2. A knot is apparently tied in the handkerchief (fig. 3). Pull the ends. The loop slides off the left wrist and the knot disappears (fig. 4). Work this trick rather rapidly, and it will completely mystify everyone.

fig. 1

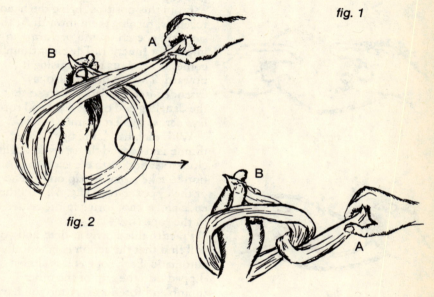

fig. 2

fig. 3

fig. 4

Quick Trick Knot

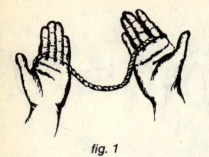

fig. 1

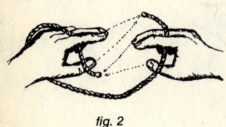

fig. 2

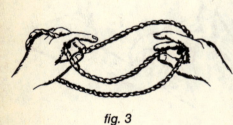

fig. 3

fig. 4

Here is a quick way of tying a knot in the center of a rope, yet apparently without releasing the ends. Something that should be utterly impossible!

Hold the right end of the rope in the right hand so it runs across the inside of the fingers and extends down between the first and second fingers. Hold the left end in the left hand so it runs behind the fingers and up between the first and second fingers (fig. 1).

From this position, bring the hand together, turning them inward. At the same time, each thumb performs an important function. The right thumb comes beneath its rope, raising it upward. The left thumb also is extended in a similar fashion so that the dangling end of the left hand rope lays across the left thumb (fig. 2).

With each hand, the tips of the thumb and second finger are brought close together, so that each is in position to take a pincer grip on the end of the opposite rope (fig. 3). Pull the ends and a knot forms in the center of the rope (fig. 4).

Practice this slowly at first, and you will find that the action is practically automatic. Each rope end is almost flipped into the grip of the other thumb and forefinger. After you have practiced the trick, you can repeat it as often as you want, always with the same baffling result.

In addition, you can make it into a Square Knot as follows: You reverse the positions of the hands, with the left holding the rope across the front of the fingers and the right having its rope in back. Then tie another Overhand Knot in the same quick manner, each hand merely working the opposite of the way it did before.

The Mysterious Ring

Your hands are tied together with a loop of string between (fig. 1). The knots are tied and sealed, if desired. Take a ring, then turn your back for a moment. When you show your hands, the ring is tied between them on the string (fig. 6).

To perform this trick, take a loop of string and push it through the center of the ring (fig. 2).

Push the loop of string up under the string encircling the wrist, and pass the loop over the fingers of the hand (figs. 3 and 4).

Then push the loop under the string in back of the wrist, and bring the loop over the fingers again (fig. 5).

As a result, the ring will be tied on the string (fig. 6). With a little practice, these movements can be performed rapidly.

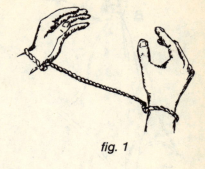

fig. 1

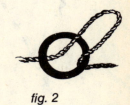

fig. 2

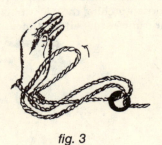

fig. 3

fig. 4

fig. 5

fig. 6

The Appearing Knot

Take a handkerchief and hold it by one corner. Shake it two or three times and suddenly a knot appears in the hanging corner of the handkerchief.

Here is how it is done: Start with a handkerchief with one corner tied in a knot. Hold it as shown in figure 1, with corner A hanging down. The corner with a knot in it (corner B) is concealed in the right hand.

Lift up corner A with the left hand, so that both corners are held in the right hand. Give the handkerchief a quick shake and let corner A fall again. Repeat this two or three times, and act disappointed when no knot appears.

The last time you take up corner A, so that you have both corners in the right hand (fig. 2), hold on to corner A when you shake the handkerchief, and let corner B fall instead. In other words, exchange the corners (fig. 3). Those watching the trick think it is the same corner all the time.

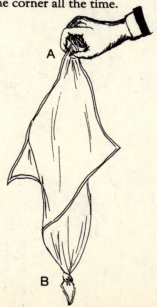

Knots that are Not

There are many knot tying tricks, some very complicated, but this one is so simple that it can easily be learned. At the same time, it appears so fair that no one will suspect trickery.

Take a piece of string and tie it in three single knots, one at a time. When you pull the ends of the string, the knots draw together, and then suddenly come apart so not a knot remains!

The first step is to tie a single knot (fig. 1). Note that end A comes nearest to the performer — in front of the knot. Then tie a similar knot, forming two loops ("X" and "Y"). Again be sure that the right end ("A") comes to the front (fig. 2). The result will be the ordinary Square Knot.

The trick lies in the third knot. Push end A through loop "X" from the front, bring it around to the front again (over top of itself), push it through loop "Y," and out behind its original position (fig. 3).

Just pull the ends and the knots will disappear.

A

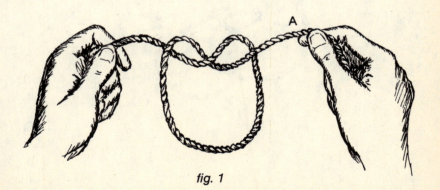

fig. 1

Learn this trick and practice it.
Once you have done it a few times,
you will never forget it, and it will
always be mystifying to those who
see it.
The trick can be performed with a
rope, a belt, or a large silk
handkerchief.

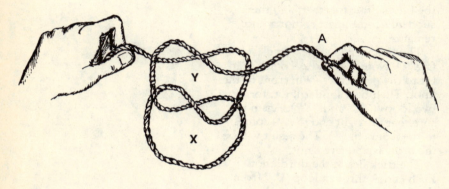

fig. 2

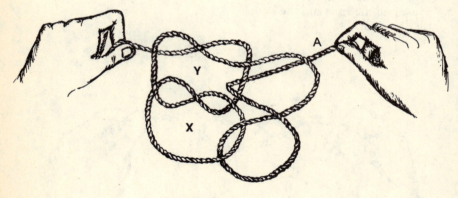

fig. 3

The Knotted Ring

As a perfect follow-up to "Knots that are Not," a bracelet or a curtain ring can be tied to the center of a cord, only to drop free when you pull the ends.

Run the cord through the ring from left to right (fig. 1). Tie a loose overhand knot above (fig. 2) and bring the right end below the ring, thrusting it through the ring as indicated by the arrow (fig. 2).

Carry the end under the cord, bring it up and push it down through the original loop as shown by the arrow (fig. 3). Pull the ends of the cord in opposite directions. The ring will drop from the cord as the knot dissolves.

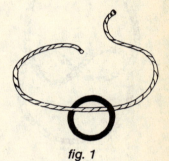

fig. 1

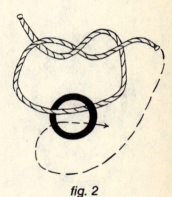

fig. 2

fig. 3

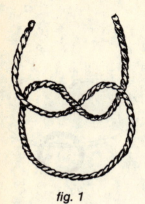

fig. 1

fig. 2

fig. 3

Trap the Knot

A neat puzzle with a two-foot length of rope.

Tie a single overhand knot (fig. 1). Then tie the ends in a tight square knot (fig. 2), trapping the single knot in the center. The trick is to remove the single knot without untying the ends (fig. 3).

The method: Turn your back and pull the sides of the lower loop outward. This forces the "trapped" single knot up into the square knot, where it remain hidden when you show the big loop.

XII

ILLUSTRATED ROPECRAFT

Illustrated Ropecraft

By following the step-by-step knot formations described in the previous chapters, the reader will develop the skills to apply to forming other knots. This means that he will be able to study finished knots and use the skills he has acquired to form his own steps toward tying them.

With this in mind, the completed knots shown in this chapter have been chosen for advanced, individual work. Some knots have been described in step-by-step procedures earlier in this book. Others are variations of established types. All offer an opportunity to develop individual skill in the field of knotcraft.

OVERHAND KNOT

SHEET BEND

STEVE DORE'S KNOT

SHEET BEND DOUBLE

OVERHAND BOW

SQUARE KNOT

SAILOR'S KNOT

CLOVE HITCH

FISHERMAN'S KNOT

128

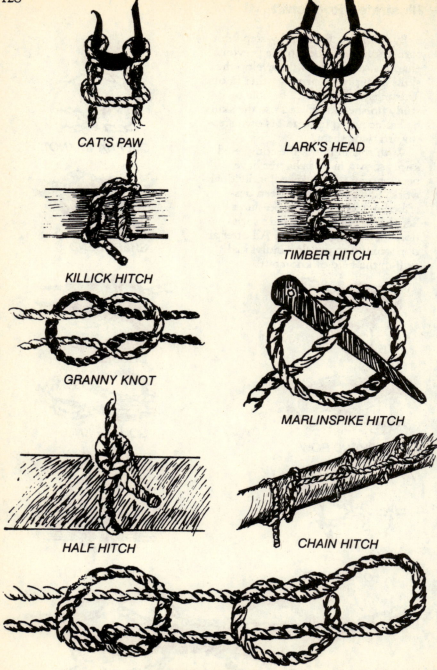

CAT'S PAW

LARK'S HEAD

KILLICK HITCH

TIMBER HITCH

GRANNY KNOT

MARLINSPIKE HITCH

HALF HITCH

CHAIN HITCH

FISHERMAN'S EYE

SLIPPERY HITCH

RUNNING KNOT

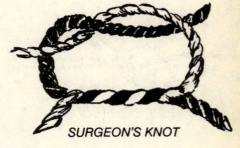

SURGEON'S KNOT

FIGURE EIGHT KNOT

ROLLING HITCH

LARIAT LOOP

CARRICK BEND

BOWLINE

**BOWLINE
ON BIGHT**

FIGURE EIGHT DOUBLE

TWO HALF HITCHES

FISHERMAN'S BEND

HALYARD BEND

BOW KNOT

MIDSHIPMAN'S HITCH

BLACKWALL HITCH

DOUBLE OVERHAND

TAUT LINE HITCH

HITCHING TIE

MILLER'S KNOT

TILLER'S HITCH

SHEEPSHANK

INDEX